THE REMARKABLE JOURNEY OF MISS TRANBY QUIRKE

ELIZABETH RIDLEY

A *Virago* Book

First published in Great Britain in 1996 by Virago Press

Copyright © 1996, Elizabeth Ridley

The moral right of the author has been asserted.

All characters in this publication are fictitious and any resemblance to real persons, living or dead, is purely coincidental.

A CIP catalogue record for this book is available
from the British Library.

ISBN 1 86049 225 8

Typeset in Palatino by M Rules
Printed and bound in Great Britain by
Clays Ltd, St Ives plc

Virago Press
A Division of
Little, Brown and Company (UK)
Brettenham House
Lancaster Place
London WC2E 7EN

For XXX – a promise kept

I would like to thank everyone who supported me during the writing of this book, especially my family – Mom, Dad, Jenny, Amy, Randy and Jim.

Thanks to my agent, Jonny Geller, and thanks to my editor, Alan Samson of Little, Brown, for picking me out of the slush pile and believing in this book from beginning to end.

Special mention to all my classmates in the MA in Creative Writing programme at the University of East Anglia; especially my tutors, Andrew Motion and Russell Celyn Jones.

Finally, thanks to my rabbit, Beryl, for always being there.

MEMORANDUM

From: The Offices of The British Society For The Aid Of
Distressed Spinsters And Gentlewomen-In-Need;
Miss Tranby Quirke, President, Camberwell Division.

LONDON, **20 September 1909**

Three o'clock in the morning

I think it would be reasonable to suggest that the strangest
and most unsettling aspect of being dead, at least in my
heretofore limited experience, is how strikingly similar it is to
being alive. By my best reckoning I have been dead for four
weeks, two days, ten hours, and twenty-seven minutes, and
very little of my existence has altered in the least. The men
and women who see me strolling through Kensington Square
ignore me as they always have. The pigeons fluttering over
my head descend only long enough to ascertain that I possess
no bread, then rise, rattle, and move on to trouble someone
else. I speak, I eat, I dream of the lives I might have had. I
marvel over roaring motorcars. I weep visible and bitter tears

that drop and dot my stiff white shirt front. Last night the bedsprings groaned beneath my body, adjusting to the shifting weight of bone, and my sharp-tipped shoulders dented the bedclothes. Even as I write these words, the candle's flame before me rises, whips, then dies at the rush of breath from my lips, and the same ink pours from my pen as always. These events and other similar phenomena might be mistaken for signs of life, but I am no longer so easily fooled. I know now that no real heart beats inside me, only a false and flimsy heart made of paper dreams and denied desires, a heart that flutters and is unreliable, keeps bad time and is doomed to wear out soon. Paper never lasts the way that flesh and blood does.

Were I a sentimental woman, I would spend my last few hours bidding tender farewells to my mementoes, my possessions, my things. I would collect my few friends as rosebuds, gather them in my loving arms and bid them all good-bye. I would sigh and fawn about my bed, the credenza, the Viennese shelves. I would pause to lament my best dresses. Letters from my late father I would clutch to my empty chest. But sentimentality was a disease I never suffered from, not even while I lived as a true-hearted being.

'Yes yes yes, I'll try to write more quickly,' I say, silencing the gibbering whispers of the angels seated on my every side, impatient to take up my body, to dress themselves in my ill-fitting skin. I can feel these creatures hovering over my shoulder, muscling each other away, dipping their fingers deep into the blackened inkwells of my hollow body. The ghosts grow stronger as the night thickens, and as they chide me, they remind me that I must hurry, I must relate this entire tale before it is too late. The last hope of my life is that this story will be sent on to Mrs McDonald, and in it she will read and believe these words, which good manners and better judgement forbade me to speak aloud: 'My darling Lysette, I'm sorry I could not love you better. May this fault be rectified by my death. I love you, I love you, I love you, Lysette.'

PART ONE

'. . . To live a barren sister all your life,
Chanting faint hymns to the cold fruitless moon.'

A Midsummer Night's Dream

CHAPTER ONE

I, Miss Tranby Quirke, have lived my whole life as an invisible woman. Of course it could be argued, I suppose, that most women are less than completely visible, or at the very least, less than evident. Certainly we are never absolute or obvious, as men may be. We women live out our lives of quiet desperation and toil in obscurity, satisfied with playing the part of shadow creatures who live in the steps behind our husbands, and in the unspoken acknowledgement for our children's achievements, and in the quiet but vital work that continues in kitchens and bedrooms and nurseries. We hope against hope to be noticed, and pray that our work will be valued and honoured somehow, somewhere, some way, even if only in private. We hold our collective breath and wait, sometimes for ever, listening for the 'yes' that will make our lives real.

This is the hidden life of most women, but my life has been less visible even than this. I was always in a hurry as I moved in and out of crowds with my head down, my mouth firm, and my steps determined. I strove to be never noticed, never seen. I was permanently dressed in widow's weeds, black shawl and black cape and broad-brimmed, black-ribboned hat, with a few beads of jet and a simple white workshirt next to my skin. And these dark garments I wore were always made of bombazine, a fabric so dull, so incapable of shining, that even one hundred candles couldn't illuminate that blackness. These were the clothes I put on to mourn my father's passing four years ago. When I discovered how well sorrow suited me, I vowed to wear black for ever, to never let go of grief, because grief was the only emotion I could openly express. I was there wearing black, in the background at the Hyde Park demonstration last Midsummer's Day. My sisters marched proudly and demanded the vote, but I opted instead to crouch in their shadows, a shadow's shadow perhaps, desperate not to be named, challenged, or seen. Instead I revived my brave colleagues with sips of weak tea, content to envy both their courage and their eye-catching regalia of purple, white, and bright green.

Although I have always prided myself on my intellect and my attention to the rational world, I do, on occasion, engage in 'automatic writing', a process which allows me to make midnight journeys through time and space in order to explore the far corners of the globe. I am not a Theosophist, a Cabalist, or even a member of the Society for Psychical Research, but two years ago I called on the famed spiritualist medium Madame Karlovsky during her visit to Dulwich, in hopes of receiving communication from the spirit of my late father. 'You do not zee your vather viz your eyes because you do not veel him in your heart,' insisted Miss Editha Saguza, the Madame's eerie, orange-skinned assistant, as she fondled my palms and blew opium smoke in my face, coaxing my father's voice to flow through my body. Sadly, I never felt my father's presence, but my single consolation has been that on that night, and on many nights since then, when I have sat down to write, strange adventures have flowed out of the ink pen in my hand, completely independent of my mind.

Until recently I taught two courses, 'The Science of Domestic Health and Hygiene', and 'Popular Thought For Modern Women' at the Simperton Institute in High Holborn. As an instructor, it was my duty to oversee the intellectual development of the young wives of middle-class business-men, to prepare them to be happy wives and healthy mothers, good hostesses, and informed conversationalists. This, my vocation, I embraced with the fervour and, I dare say, utter seriousness befitting a woman of my social standing; my standing being that of a thirty-four-year-old unmarried woman with a small independency from my late father's pension; a private flat above Hambleton's Bakery Shop in Camberwell; and as good an education as could be had by one of my gender. I was stern and I was moral; a dull lecturer, I'm certain, but in possession of both a clear, well-modulated speaking voice, and the absolute and unshakeable belief that women have a right to be educated. Of course, I know that when I say 'educated', I must define my terms. Left to my own devices, I would have taught my girls serious subjects; science, mathematics, classics, and my personal passion, the history of discovery and global exploration. But the Simperton Institute was ruled by a Board of Governors made up of many prominent citizens including one bishop, a baronet, and three knights, according to whom the purpose of the Institute was, 'to provide a sheltered and protected envi-ronment in which refined young ladies may receive quality tuition in the gentle and feminine arts of cooking, household management, childrearing, and personal presentation'.

The full extent to which the governors adhered to this state-ment of purpose can be best illustrated by the 'Wall of Female

Achievers' incident. During my first week of teaching at the Institute, I had decided to decorate my draughty little classroom with portraits of successful women, as a means of inspiring my girls to achieve great things. Well, no sooner had I finished positioning Jane Austen than our Headmaster, Mr Cyril Westonbury, barrelled into the classroom and considered the wall with solemn and fearful looks. After much squinting and straining, hemming and hawing, and extensive patting of his considerable girth, Mr Westonbury told me, 'I can't see any harm in making examples of these women, Miss Quirke, but to be fair, you must present a more balanced picture. Do not be afraid to show also the unsung heroines, the brave everyday English wives and mothers. After all, they are the true saviours of our nation and our Empire, and they play their part silently, not asking for notice or attention, or vulgarly expecting to have their names and their exploits published in newspapers.'

I tried to offer him a facial response of temperance and grave regret, but by the time I had my features properly placed, he had turned and walked away. Having no other choice, I redesigned the wall, and the result was rather ironic – a 'Wall of Female Achievers' in which Emily Brontë, novelist, sat opposite Lady Augusta Halliday, society wife; and Dr Elizabeth Garrett Anderson, medical pioneer, challenged Mrs Warburton Trimble; and just beneath her, Florence Nightingale, heroic war nurse, icily eyed her adversary, Mrs Jane Stanfield-Jones, devoted wife and mother of seven.

In addition to my work as an instructor, I was, unbeknownst to most of my colleagues and students, and even many of my friends, a private crusader – a secret suffragette.

'Miss Quirke, do you support the tenets of the suffragist campaign?' I was asked during an open meeting on my first day at the Simperton Institute. The Institute was still recovering from a bad experience with a suffragette instructor who had gone on hunger strike and fainted during a lecture on general nutrition, which caused a terrible scene and cast the entire establishment in a very bad light.

'No, sir, I most definitely do not support the suffragist movement. My devotion to my students keeps me far too busy to engage in such frivolities,' I had answered staunchly before taking my seat. But in truth, for many years I have held, or perhaps it would be more proper to say I had held, for it is questionable whether the dead can really hold opinions, the rather radical conviction that women should be granted the right to vote; a right freely given to drunkards, imbeciles, and inveterate gamblers, not to mention Members of Parliament. I can see no logical reason why women shouldn't be allowed to practise medicine, own property, be granted custody of their own children, and divorce unfaithful husbands.

Oh, I must insist that I always scrupulously avoided scandal. I was never a law-breaker. I never believed it necessary to be so extreme. I never threw bricks through shop windows on Bond Street; I had no intention of disrupting the election of Mr Winston Churchill as a candidate for Manchester; and I never chained myself to the railing at Number 10 Downing Street. My most radical action took place when I participated in a public reading of Elizabeth Barrett Browning poems outside Holloway Prison, in support of our sisters in police custody beneath us who were, I'm told, being subjected to unspeakable indecencies in their damp and draughty cells.

To be completely candid, I must also acknowledge that my involvement with women goes beyond educating them, and securing the right to vote. Like a silent spring, my interest flows deeper than this. The lives, the loves, the troubles; the hats, the husbands, the petty complaints of other women, these are the things that have always been of utmost concern to me, the thoughts that most brightened my life.

Let me assure you here and now, I am not vulgar. I have never been predatory. No one could accuse me of being indiscreet. But I am what is referred to as, during the rare instances in which it is referred to at all, a 'homo-sexual', or an 'invert', or, in the most recent parlance, a 'lesbian'.

My first and only encounter of this kind came at the age of twelve, when I travelled to Bournemouth with my father, where he was attending a conference to give a lecture on advances in the treatment of tuberculosis. Perhaps I need to digress here to tell a bit about my childhood. I was a shy and bookish girl who rarely strayed from her father's side. Although my very early years had been filled with illnesses – pneumonia, pleurisy, and croup, among others, by the time I was nine or ten I had completely recovered my health. Still, Father insisted on educating me at home to spare my being exposed to the illnesses of other children. I believe he blamed himself for my mother's death from pneumonia. When she first became ill he told her not to fuss, it was only a minor chest complaint, and that fresh air and housework would do her good. Two weeks later, she was dead. I was four years old at the time.

Father managed his grief and guilt by taking obsessively good care of me. I was not allowed to bathe on windy days, not allowed to eat anything grown outside of England, not allowed to drink tea until I was twenty-one years old. But I was a happy child with a passion for books, maps, and anatomy diagrams. I had a talent for geometry and had memorised the Latin names of fish, flowers, and birds. My world was tightly pressed and cloistered, but full of love and learning, and a string of old governesses, most of whom were relieved of their duties once Father determined that I had exhausted their stores of knowledge.

On our first day in Bournemouth, Father instructed me to explore the woods behind the hotel while he attended his lecture. He asked me to bring back some Fuller's Teasel and some Ladies' Smock, which we would examine after supper. I was heading towards the river, deeply engrossed in investigating the grasses, when I heard a shout in the distance. I knelt down and crept closer, peering over the brush that led down to the water. Beneath me I saw a creature unlike anything I had ever seen before – a Puck-like child who appeared to be part deer, part spirit, part goat. She was bare-chested and wore a boy's short trousers, two sizes too big and tied round the waist with a length of ragged string. She swung across the river on a rope, and when she slipped and fell in, she splashed back on to the bank, laughing and struggling to catch her breath.

She looked so much like a boy, a boy in every respect, but the slight swelling of her breasts, the indentation of her waist and the high pitch of her laughter insisted she was a girl. Her sandy-blonde hair had been cut short as a shepherd boy's, and stuck out in points around her ears. She had light brown eyes and lots of freckles, and her teeth were widely spaced and prominent, giving her a lop-sided grin. Her hands and feet were large and bony, her neck too long, and I knew immediately that she was not beautiful in any conventional sense, but it was too late for such a judgement, for I had already decided to make her mine.

As I inched closer, my foot dislodged a stone which tumbled down the rise. 'Who's that?' she asked, grabbing a stick and turning around. 'Who goes there?' I held my breath and leaned backwards. The branch I balanced on gave way, and I slipped out of the thicket and tumbled to the ground. I sat in the sand dazed and wounded, afraid I'd broken something vital. I was not, like most children, accustomed to falling. At the age of twelve, I don't think I had ever been bruised.

The girl was at my side in an instant, lifting me to my feet and brushing away the dirt. My legs quivered beneath me and I started to cry. The girl began to laugh. First just a giggle, but then a deep, rough belly laugh that made her whole body shake. The muscles rippled in her stomach, and as she leaned forward, I could see the notches of her spine. 'What is so amusing?' I asked, angry, although still hurt.

'You. You are so funny,' she said, unable to catch her breath. 'You look like someone's maiden aunt.' She pointed to my starched blue dress, my double stockings, my sensible hat and matching gloves. 'It's the middle of summer! What must you look like in January?' she asked.

'I don't take kindly to insults,' I told her sternly. I wanted to pull away from her, but I tingled where she touched my arm.

'I'm sorry. I know it's rude to laugh. But you look so silly! My name is Jonnie and I'm from London,' she said, bowing deeply, touching her forehead and chest in a mocking gesture that made me smile.

'Jonnie? But you're not a boy,' I said.

'No, but I want to be one. Boys are allowed to have so much more fun!' Her eyes lit up. 'My name is Virginia Appleby. Ginnie, for short, although I prefer to be called Jonnie.'

'My name is Tranby Quirke. I'm from London too,' I told her.

'Tranby? That sounds like a boy's name. We could both be boys together,' she said with certainty.

'I suppose so,' I answered, considering the possibility.

'Of course, if you wanted to be a boy you would have to be able to swing on that rope,' she said, pointing across the water.

'I could do that,' I said quickly, knowing full well that I couldn't.

She squinted her eye at me. 'I doubt it. Still, you could try.'

'I'm not as weak as I look,' I challenged her.

'Prove it,' she said, gesturing to the rope. I approached the river's edge and reached out on tiptoe, stretching as far as I could. The rope was still an inch out of my grasp. I looked over my shoulder at Jonnie. Her arms were folded across her narrow chest as she leaned nonchalantly against a tree. 'That's the way. You've almost got it,' she said. I pressed a hair-breadth closer and felt a clump of earth break beneath my foot. I lost my balance and slipped into the water. My stockings and skirt filled quickly, ballooning out around me, and I struggled to stand up. I kicked and thrashed, but the harder I fought the deeper I sank, until I felt my legs tire and catch in the thick sinewy rushes.

Just as I felt myself give up, Jonnie's strong arm was around my waist, pulling me to shore. I felt the pebbles scratch my back as she dragged me to safety. 'Tranby, Tranby, please be all right,' she said as she stroked my hands. Water streamed from my stockings and sleeves. My head was spinning and I jerked forward in a spasm of coughing. Jonnie helped me to sit forward and slapped my back. Water continued to pour from every part of me, and as I opened my eyes I saw my hat floating darkly downstream. 'Are you all right?' Jonnie asked. Her eyes were huge and dark and her voice rattled in her throat.

I nodded, unable to speak. 'Oh, I'm so glad!' she exclaimed, throwing her arms around me and kissing me full on the mouth.

'What was that?' I asked, recovered from my near-drowning, but shocked by her kiss.

She blushed. 'I was kissing you. Haven't you ever been kissed before?' she asked.

I thought about my endless progression of aunts who, every holiday, pulled me to their bosoms and brushed their lips against my cheek. 'No,' I said.

Her expression was serious, but she had a gleam in her eye. 'I must warn you, kissing can be difficult,' she said. 'It's only for very brave girls. Will you kiss me?'

'Yes,' I said, not wanting to seem a coward. I made a futile pass at her face, but I ducked away at the last moment, uncertain where to place my lips. She kissed me instead and I nearly fainted from the thrill.

'That wasn't so bad, was it?' she said and laughed.

'No, it was fine,' I answered, once I had caught my breath. I saw a future before me of potential kisses, each one opening like a rose.

For the remainder of the afternoon, we sat in the grass, talking and waiting for my stockings to dry. The sun was warm and generous, and Jonnie told me about her life, her stern parents, her older brothers. I told her all about myself, my love for books, my interest in explorers. When the sun began to dip behind the trees, Jonnie announced that it was time for her to leave.

'Meet me here tomorrow at midday,' she said, squeezing my hand in her long bony fingers. 'And I promise I will teach you how to swing on the rope.' Her broad smile split her face into two shining half-moons.

'I'll try,' I said. 'I have to sneak away from my governess.'

'Well, try your very best,' she said as we stood to leave. She began skipping backwards, waving and saluting as she danced away. When she was out of my view, I turned to walk back to the hotel. 'I love you, Tranby,' she called out after me. Her words seemed to vibrate above my head, spreading like a secret between the trees. Her voice echoed in the air, drifting higher and higher, but never quite disappearing.

When I returned to the hotel I found Mrs Dudley, my governess, fanning herself on the veranda with a large box of chocolates by her side. 'Oh, Tranby, I was just resting my eyes and I didn't know where you were. Now, you weren't causing any trouble, were you?'

'No, Mrs Dudley. But I slipped into the river while I was looking for a water lily.'

Her eyelids dipped open sleepily as she considered my rumpled stockings. 'It shouldn't be a problem. We'll have those ironed straight away and they should be fine. Very good girl. I shall tell your father what a lovely child you've been,' she said, as her eyes slipped back under their heavily protective lids.

That night I could barely sleep for the excitement of seeing Jonnie. Even the simplest activities, brushing my hair, cleaning my teeth, sliding into my nightgown, felt new and unusual. The bedsheets smelled of strangers, and rattling music rose from the hotel ballroom, complemented by the clatter of dishes dancing in the kitchens. When Father came in to wish me good-night, I wanted to ask him every question about love, but I didn't dare say a word.

'Good-night, Tranby', he said.

'Good-night, Father', I answered. I smiled in the dark and let Jonnie's kiss be a secret between us.

The next morning I was awakened by the sound of commotion on the floors of the hotel beneath us. Father was gone. I asked Mrs Dudley what had happened. 'There's been an accident by the river. No one knows quite what's happened,' she said.

A sick feeling tugged at my insides. *Please, God, let Jonnie be all right, let Jonnie be all right. Let her have left several hours ago. Let her be thirty miles closer to London, far from whatever sorrow is about to fall.* I pulled off my nightgown, threw on a dress and ran all the way down to the river. A crowd had gathered on the bank. I pushed through the people and saw my father, standing in a few inches of water, leaning over a bloated blue body with a cap of dark hair. I rejoiced. It was not Jonnie. It couldn't be. The body was too big, too heavy. Too blue . . . I screamed. Father looked up and his eyes found me in the crowd. He let the body slip from his arms and he rushed over to me. 'Tranby, run back to the hotel,' he said evenly. I was paralysed, unable to think or breathe. 'I have never raised my voice to you before, but I am ordering you now, go back to the hotel.' I tried to fight out of his grip, but he pressed my face into his shoulder and would not let me see. 'Go back now – this is no sight for a child.' I heard a tremor in his chest and I was terrified that he might weep. Dutifully I nodded. 'That's a good girl,' he whispered huskily. 'Go now, please,' he said, and such was my determination not to see him cry that I turned and ran back to the hotel, thinking if I ran fast enough I could turn back the earth, Father would not weep, and I would find Jonnie waiting for me, smiling her lop-sided grin.

When I reached the hotel, I collapsed on the steps and drew my knees up into my chest. My lips tingled and I felt a rip opening up in my heart. So this is love, I told myself. This is love.

When Father returned from the river, I wanted to run to him, throw my arms around him and bury my head in his embrace. I wanted him to stroke my head and promise me all would be well, but I held back, drew in my tears and straightened my shoulders. I had entered a strange new world. I understood that I was past the point of sympathy now, and silence was the price I would pay for having loved Jonnie.

When Father reached me, he looked solemn and worn. He put his hand on my shoulder and lowered himself to sit beside me. For a long time we said nothing, and his ragged breathing was the only sound I heard. 'She was my friend, Father,' I said eventually. 'I disobeyed you. I left the hotel yesterday and I went to play with her, with that girl, by the river.' My throat ached, but I had finished with tears.

'I am so sorry, Tranby,' he said, grasping my hand.

'How did it happen?' I asked.

'I'm not certain,' he said with a deep sigh. 'The family say she slipped into the river. I suppose we will never know the truth.' He put his arm around me and held me so close I could smell the tobacco in his pocket and feel the ticking of his watch. 'A waste of a young life,' he whispered bitterly. He didn't know what had happened, but I did. She had died because of loving me. I felt my heart eclipse itself and slip into a deep, dark shadow where it would beat quietly, always aware of its wound.

That evening Father ordered an elaborate supper of roast beef with turnips and gravy, but neither of us could eat a morsel. In the middle of the meal, Father threw down his silverware and announced that we would return to London. He hadn't yet given his lecture, but the sadness, the silence, and the curiosity which pervaded the hotel was more than he could bear. We had missed the last train of the day, so he called for a coach and driver to fly us back to London, and Father impatiently loaded all our luggage into the carriage himself, calling to the driver to make haste in preparing the horses.

Father helped me up the step and we huddled on the wooden seat, wrapped in an unnecessary blanket, for the evening was warm and humid and still and the air dared to smell of jasmine and lavender. I could see people through the hotel windows and on the veranda, talking and smoking, and I imagined they were already making a myth of the drowned little girl, telling how she had been found shirtless and bruised, floating face down on the river. The driver cracked his whip and the carriage lurched forward. Father stroked my hair and smoked his pipe, muttering beneath his breath, 'Faster, faster, faster.' The driver sped through the night, whipping the horses at a furious pace, but still Father goaded him, pushing him to pick up speed. The road was dark and rough and the ride so violent that my bones ground against each other. I longed to cry out, but I held my tongue and let the pain echo in my skull. *I will never love, never love, never love.* The words ached in my blood, beating against my heart and liver and lungs, until I felt my insides puff and swell, pushing to the surface of my skin.

'Can you please pick up the speed!' Father pleaded with the driver. 'We must reach London as quickly as possible.' Then he tried to comfort me. 'Don't despair, Tranby, we will be home soon,' he said. 'Home safe and sound, where we shall put all this sadness behind us.' Father thought we could fly death, but death was everywhere. Death kept pace; it lay in wait around each bend in the road; it was a black cloak fluttering behind us, death was in the wind at the horses' hooves and conspiring high in the night sky; death spread through us like a dreadful rumour whispered in our ears by hawks and bats and owls.

And so I grew to womanhood determined not to love again. The struggle was difficult when I was younger, but as I grew older, the tension eased. The number of girls who tried to win my passionate friendship was fewer and fewer every year, until, by my early twenties, they seemed to disappear completely. I channelled all my energy into teaching, into suffragism, into the idea of changing the world in my own significant, but very small, way. I considered my orientation to be a flaw of an almost Classical nature. I learned to ignore

the charms of womanhood, and not to wonder what might be
hiding beneath the elaborate hats, the padded coiffures, the
layers of petticoats and those long trailing skirts. I was pure
in action, if not always in thought. Desires could be mas-
tered, I was living proof of that. And I had retained my
steadfastness. At least until I met Lysette, and along with her
came my headlong descent into a swift, violent, and self-
inflicted death.

Release me from my misery, Lysette McDonald. I read and re-
read the note hastily pressed into my hand by the one-eyed
messenger girl.

'Are you absolutely certain this note was meant for me?' I
asked her again.

'Most certainly it is,' the girl insisted. I had been returning
to my office after a lecture on dry rot removal. It was the
fourth of March of this year, and there were no other signs
that my life was about to change in so significant a way.
Release me from my misery. Misery? Lysette McDonald? Was it
her personal misery that was at issue here, or was someone
else naming her as the source of their own misery? I racked
my brain. Lysette McDonald? She had been a student of mine
for several months. Not a brilliant scholar, but she had always
seemed to be a charming, cheerful girl who possessed a spark
of youthful exuberance which many of my other students
lacked, especially those students who enjoyed the benefit of
six or more months of holy matrimony.

Misery? Lysette McDonald? The thought troubled me.
What misery could she know, she in her emerald green velvet
dresses and her cream-coloured silk gloves buttoned up to
her elbows? She was no more than nineteen years old, and
unusually beautiful, but definitely not of the best breeding.
She was the sort of woman I normally treated with derision

or, at the very least, mild disdain. I was told she had married a commercial traveller in Hampstead who was moving up the social scale. I imagined he thought of her as a pretty ornament, something he could show off at summer garden parties, or introduce to his department head as physical proof of his exquisitely fine taste and more than abundant manhood.

'Very well then,' I told myself as I read the note again. 'Tranby Quirke, you have embarked on a new adventure, without ever so much as setting sail. You shall uncover the source of this mysterious misery.'

When Lysette McDonald next attended my class on 'Popular Thought for Modern Women', I slipped this note into her hand: *Mrs McDonald, I would be happy to meet with you at half four this afternoon, during my regular office hours, to discuss the matter of your progress in this course. With kind regards, your instructor, Miss Tranby Quirke.*

One might not surmise, simply by reading the note, that in truth I agonised over those words for ages, tore up the paper and re-wrote it a dozen times. I worried – was it too familiar? Too austere? Was it obvious from the shaky lettering that this young lady had achieved something which no one had done for years – she had captured my fancy and begun to toy with my imagination.

My lecture that day concerned Darwin's 'The Origin of Species', and the case for and against the use of powdered milk in suckling infants. This was a straightforward, somewhat boring lecture, not burdened down with a surfeit of facts. I tried to underline, as always, the moral rectitude of progress, the truth and beauty of a woman's noble duty to her household, and highlight the good fortune we have to live in such a sensible nation as England, where things are discovered just at the moment they are most likely to prove useful. My students listened and wrote copious notes as always, but I was hardly at the peak of my form. Mrs McDonald, sitting as usual in the third row, second from the left, was watching me intently; pouring out at me a look of serene composure, of interest and complete absorption, not in the subject matter itself, but in my presentation of it. I stumbled once, and twice had to begin a sentence again. My voice dried and my knees shook. I thought I caught her winking at me. That thin sliver of an eyelid, dipping enticingly over that eye. My heart stuttered at her boldness and her beauty. 'Charles Durwood,' I heard myself stammer, 'I'm sorry, I mean Darwin.' Her eyes peeled away my epidermis like the skins of an onion. She saw the confusion that gripped my soul and stirred my nerve endings. A deep heat crept up the back of my neck, and a knot swelled my throat so that I could scarcely take in air.

Resist this beauty, Tranby, resist it with all your might, I warned myself, *as if it were the devil himself*. But then Mrs McDonald smiled secretly, a smile as deft and darting as a little Christmas ribbon, unwinding around her lip as it tightened around my heart. I put on the armour of a serious lecturer. I steeled my gaze, stiffened my shoulders and mapped out my theories with fresh chalk firmly in hand. But to no avail. Arrows shot from Mrs McDonald's eyes and fixed on mine, striking my skull before sliding into my bloodstream. Her interested, excited eyes followed my body up and down and up and down. She peered behind my quivering ribs and marked my fluttering heart as it grew thin and blistered from overwork, and I was ashamed that she was forced to endure the sight of my distressed intestines, twisting around my stomach, mixing a sour, fluidy brew. I was terrified I might lose my bearings and burp out strange words, or become a jiggling jelly, and my students would have to lift me in cupfuls off the floor, after I had been made all spooney and ruined by lust.

I ended the lecture when my lungs ran out of air and the faces of my students had been diluted to a dizzy whirl. The girls, who were pleased to be leaving a quarter hour early, filed out of the classroom one by one, in the deferential yet elegant manner in which they had been instructed. Mrs McDonald, as she approached the door, paused briefly and glanced back at me, smiling over her shoulder.

I returned to the third floor of the Simperton Institute where, since the sudden death of my dear colleague Miss Philomena Tapp-Andrews, I had private use of a spacious corner office that smelled of tallow candles and ginger biscuits and paraffin, and featured two tall glass casement windows, one with a thin crack through the middle of it. I stood beside the window, close enough to the crack that the draught whispered against my breast and rattled my ribs. I watched the rain weep and bead steadily against the glass, obscuring my view but softening the rough edges of London. I did not mind the rain, but I cherished the rare clear days, days when the fog parted and I had visions of chimneypots and rooftops and high church spires somewhere miles north of London, but just within dreaming distance. I pressed my hands against the window and felt a sudden flutter beneath my skin. When I stepped back and touched the glass again, the sensation was gone. My thoughts returned to Mrs McDonald. In a few hours, I told myself, we will feast on her misery.

'Miss Quirke, Miss Persildown has asked me to inquire whether she might borrow your lecture notes regarding the Boer War.' This booming voice, like a soldier's call to arms, interrupted my reverie. I turned towards Miss Wilhelmina Fickle, our needlework teacher of rotund proportions, who stood in the doorway bouncing a set of books squarely against her ample hips.

Suddenly I felt flustered, and my neatly coiled hair seemed to stand up in pinpoints on my scalp. 'Of course,' I said as I ruffled through the pile of papers on my desk. 'I had every intention of giving them to her this morning. Do offer my apologies.' I held up the loose file, which Miss Fickle squarely snatched away from me. She turned to leave, pausing only long enough to grunt a good-bye before rolling like a storm cloud down the hallway.

'So silly of me to forget,' I chided myself. 'What could I have been thinking?' My hands felt cold, and as I turned them over they looked pale and ghostly, as if kept alive only by the thin vein running beneath the skin. I watered my only office plant, an unremarkable philodendron, then sat at my desk with my knees trembling. *This can not be happening. This can not be happening to me; not at my age. Mrs McDonald? This could not be happening to me.* My pocket watch read half eleven. The students had a midday break, during which most went to the local tea rooms for a meal, and then returned for their afternoon lectures. This meant enduring five hours until Mrs McDonald would appear.

I looked around the room, wondering if it was worth the trouble of attempting to tidy up. My office, although comfortable, was terribly messy – full of several pairs of scissors, newspaper clippings, crumbled biscuits, haphazard maps, and a glass case of carefully preserved rare South American insects. Two broken umbrellas guarded the doorway, propping it up on either side like wounded soldiers. Somewhere beneath all the clutter hid two beautiful globes, a terrestrial and a celestial, and an aquatint of Christopher Columbus landing in San Salvador, but I had not seen these items for several weeks. Ironically, I dared to preach order and neatness almost like a fifth Gospel. 'A husband, after a hard day of working, appreciates a tidy, well-kept home . . .' How often had I begun a lecture with those very words?

Rather than tidy up, I sat down to do some book work. While I busied myself correcting students' papers, deducting several points for poor penmanship, I was aware of time passing. I could feel it in the ticking movements of my father's watch which was, as always, strung so tight to my workshirt that it beat against my ribs. 'Pass faster, pass faster,' I whispered, as if my words could speed those steady movements. The flutter of the small black hands reminded me of Mrs McDonald winking, and I saw the flutter of her long black lashes, beating quick against those gleaming cheeks.

After I finished my book work I caught up on a little mending I'd brought from home, and toyed with some new suffrage slogans, but still it was not time to meet Mrs McDonald. Giving myself leave to indulge in my favourite hobby, I opened my *National And World Gazetteer* to the map of Africa and I traced Henry Morton Stanley's route to his fateful rendezvous in 1871 with David Livingstone in Ujiji. This was a route I myself undertook so often in my midnight automatic writings, but today, slipped between Africa's nearly equal, heart-shaped halves was the note that whispered in swirling, girlish handwriting, *Release me from my misery, Lysette McDonald*. What could this letter mean? I fantasised about escaping to the Congo, or floating in an open boat down the languid, turquoise Nile, lined on either side with waving palms and smiling lovers. I heard the echo of Stanley's words in my ear: 'Dr Livingstone, I presume? . . . Lysette McDonald, I presume?' The romance of those words, the handshake, the door of discovery opening on more adventure than either one of them had ever imagined . . .

A confident knock on the open door ended my reverie as

Lysette McDonald, glittering with raindrops, stepped into my office. I wanted to stand and greet her with a firm and certain handshake, but I did not trust my body to respond to my brain's conflicting commands. Mrs McDonald was wearing a huge hat with stiff silk roses, long white gloves and a short bolero jacket that emphasised the breadth of her square shoulders, in contrast to her delicate, sylph-like waist. She was a tall girl, I noted, much taller than she seemed in class. I thought she must be five and three-quarters feet tall, perhaps a little taller.

'Miss Quirke, may I see you now?' she asked, in a sweet voice smoothed over with a studied, affected diction, as if she were trying to hide a provincial accent.

'Why yes, of course, Mrs McDonald. Do come in and sit down. I was very concerned when I received your message.' I stood and motioned to the small wooden chair in front of my desk.

A smile darted across her broad face, but then she frowned, withdrawing the smile and pursing her lips as she gathered the folds of her skirt and carefully lowered herself to the chair. I wanted to scream out, *'Smile, dear girl, smile. Feel free to smile as much as you please. Nothing could so illuminate these dull office walls.'*

'Thank you very much, Miss Quirke,' she said and wiped her forehead with the back of her white-gloved hand. She glanced around my office, admiring the many maps and exploration pictorials displayed on the walls. 'New Guinea. Australia. Tasmania. Well, those are certainly some faraway places,' she said. 'I wish I could go away somewhere. I would love to travel and see a bit of the world.'

'As would I,' I replied, delighted that we had this interest in common. I picked up the copy of *The Times* folded on the edge of my desk and brushed away some seedcake crumbs. 'Have you been following the Robert Peary expedition? What a fantastic adventure, to search for the North Pole!'

I held out the paper to her and she casually glanced over it, dismissing it with a barely visible tilt of her head. 'Must be frightfully cold all the way up there; he's a brave chap for having a go at it. I don't read newspapers at home. Mr McDonald says there's nothing in the newspaper that I need concern myself about,' she explained. She must have caught the glint of disappointment in my eyes. 'But I do love to read,' she interjected quickly.

'Oh, I am pleased to hear that. What sort of things do you like to read?' I asked

'Oh, novels!' she answered enthusiastically.

My spirits, already soaring, lifted higher still. 'Well, we've something else in common then, Mrs McDonald. Which authors do you enjoy – Dickens? George Eliot? Jane Austen?' I asked, listing my own personal favourites.

She lifted one eyebrow. 'Those are fine books of course, but to my mind they can't compare to romance novels. *Martha At The Bubbling Brook*, and *Incident At A Spanish Mansion*, and *Emma Hargreaves, The Saga Of A Country Lass In London*. I love to read about beautiful ladies and handsome men, and the lovely houses they live in. Makes a girl dream about all the excitement in the world.' Her eyes lit up and her slim fingers danced as she described her readings, and the lace flounce at her neck waved in rapid agreement. I resisted the urge to feel superior. I had never read a romance novel, nor did I ever intend to. Romance had no place in my life, but it was rumoured that Mrs Pankhurst herself often relied on light-weight romantic novels to cheer her spirits when imprisoned, so I saw no reason to condemn Mrs McDonald for enjoying the same entertainment as our illustrious leader.

'I was awake past midnight reading the last one!' Mrs

McDonald confided, half-embarrassed, half-triumphant, holding her white-gloved hand to her chin as a soft blush spread through her face. I smiled in spite of myself. I sensed that Mrs McDonald's background was not yet bred out; she had the firm bones, the quick smile, and the strong lungs of a North Country farm girl, accustomed to physical labour and the life out-of-doors. Although undeniably beautiful, she was somewhat unrefined; more Yorkshire heather than Devon rose. Her skin was ruddy, with high colour in the cheeks, and a smattering of freckles across her forehead; the result, no doubt, of a carefree youth, recklessly spent in the sun. Her eyes were unusual; a sharp, pungent, not-quite-ripe green. Her lips were generous; perhaps too generous, and quite red in colour, although not the gaudy, artificial red of lip salve or cosmetics, but a true-to-life red resulting from some excitement stirring in her blood. My own blood swam madly at this thought, filling me with wonder. Clearly, I could not let her continue.

'Mrs McDonald, your letter concerned me. Is there something with which you need my help?'

Her eyes narrowed briefly and her teeth caught the edge of her lip. 'It's my husband, Miss Quirke. He beats me. Even on the Sabbath.'

I was too shocked to respond. What sort of obscene and heartless creature could bear to hurt this lovely young girl? I felt oddly off-balance, as if I might laugh and cry and then crumple up like a piece of used blotting paper. I straightened some papers on my desk as Ujiji drifted off into the distance.

'Oh dear, Mrs McDonald, I am so sorry to hear that. How unfortunate,' I said, trying to be kind.

'Don't be sorry. Offer to help me. Tell me what to do. May I divorce him?' she asked hopefully, and without a shred of self-pity.

'I doubt it. Under the Matrimonial Causes Act of 1857, you would have to prove that he committed adultery, in addition to cruelty, desertion, bestiality . . .'

'Beating me is not cause enough?' she asked.

'No. It is not,' I answered truthfully.

'I feared that might be the case. Well then, tell me how to have his child,' she asked intently.

This request took me aback. 'Why ever would you want a child by this man?' I asked in disbelief. 'Forgive me, Mrs McDonald, but your husband hardly sounds as if he would prove to be a model father.'

'For one very good reason, Miss Quirke. If I have a child, I'm certain he will cease his beatings. We have been trying for a child for over a year now. Malcolm claims to beat me from disappointment. Please tell me what to do.'

'Mrs McDonald, this is hardly a subject on which I have much experience—'

She interrupted me. 'Please, Miss Quirke! You must have an answer. You're so clever, so confident . . . so like a man, if I may say that. Strong in the way a man should be, that's what I mean . . .'

I hesitated a moment, caught off-guard by her brash familiarity. The walls of my office shook as someone downstairs began calling on the taps to produce hot water.

'Please help me, Miss Quirke. I come to you because you are the only person I feel I can trust.' I could see the confusion and fear brimming in her bright green eyes. She was nearly in tears as she pressed the handkerchief to her face and blew her nose with all the force in her body. The sensible part of my brain was disgusted by the thought of publicly discussing a subject of such delicacy. And yet, in some nearly forsaken corner of my soul, I longed to take her in my arms and soothe the sorrow out of her lithe young body. I wanted to hold her close to my face and assure her all would be well. But I retained my composure. *Imagine this is the devil himself, come to tempt you,* I thought. *Resist this beauty, Tranby, resist it with all your might. As thou wouldst fly death . . .*

I cleared my throat and pressed my high white collar close to my skin. 'Mrs McDonald, forgive me, but I must ask, have you consulted a physician about your, about your situation?' I asked gently.

'Aye! I mean, yes, I have,' she said carefully. 'Malcolm has sent me to the best physicians in the city. But you know what those ladies' physicians are like . . .'

I didn't. My well-preserved purity had spared me that indecency. Other than my monthly interruptions, I lived my life as if my private parts didn't exist. I had no use for those disagreeable organs. But I had heard horror stories about what other women were forced to endure, how some were induced into nervous illness by the endless examinations; some were forcibly strapped to a table, then poked, prodded, and inspected, while others had had their organs isolated and painted with carbolic acid. So much distress endured simply for the sake of pleasuring their husbands and peopling the earth. 'Yes, Mrs McDonald, and what precisely did the physician advise?'

She took a deep breath before continuing. 'He gave me a good going-over and he said I was in sound condition . . .'

My imagination fastened on that physician. Did he appreciate how fortunate he was to have touched this woman? To have pressed his fingers into her yielding flesh, to have examined her abdominal region, to have listened to the rhythm of her heartbeat and the rumble of air in her lungs . . .

'. . . and that if I were not so headstrong, I should certainly be expecting by the end of the year,' she said, releasing a huge breath and nervously fidgeting with the cuff of her glove.

I let her breath hang in the air a moment, then I imagined it touching me, coming down to rest softly across my shoulders like a cashmere wrap. I shuffled the papers on my desk, pretending to be very busy. 'Well, Mrs McDonald, I'm not certain what to suggest, but I will try to help you. My father, the late Septimus Everdene Quirke, was a member of the Royal London College of Physicians, and when he died, I inherited his books, which I like to read in my rare spare time. It will not be too much trouble to do some research into the subject of conception.' I glanced at my calendar, discreetly marked with yellow circles to represent my secret suffrage meetings. 'Shall we meet again on the eleventh of March to discuss my findings?' I asked.

'Oh yes. Yes, Yes!' Her face lit up in a rough blush, as a fall of freckles spread across her high-bridged nose. 'Oh, thank you. Thank you, thank you, thank you!' she blurted out, jumping from the chair and reaching across the desk to shake my hand. 'I knew you'd help me. I simply knew it!'

I held her handshake as tremors of excitement surged up my arm and threatened to overthrow my throat. 'I can't promise anything, Mrs McDonald, other than to assure you that I shall do my best,' I said evenly, slipping my hand out of her grip.

'I never doubted you. No, not for a moment, Miss Quirke. I knew you would help me.'

I felt suddenly hot and out of sorts. Mrs McDonald loomed before me like a spectral vision, a waking dream that tempted me, enticing me to seize and taste and touch. I felt sheer relief when I freed her from my imagination and led her out of my office and down the corridor with my hand, damp but firm, on the velvet edge of her elbow. But then my mind shifted again, so that when we reached the top of the staircase I was overwhelmed with feelings of protectiveness, even possessiveness. I wanted to turn her towards me and stare at her face for long moments, I wanted to memorise the shape of her eyes and the set of her nose, I wanted to carve her image on my eyelid to keep me company during the long cold night ahead. I wanted to walk down the rickety wooden staircase by her side, holding her steady until she had safely reached the street, where I could squeeze her hand and kiss her cheek, and wave farewell until her image disappeared, and she had been absorbed into the crowd like a beautiful flower, hidden in the richest of gardens.

'Thank you, Miss Quirke,' she said, bobbing down the staircase that creaked for joy beneath her feet. 'I shan't sleep for excitement while waiting to see you again.'

'Do be careful, Mrs McDonald, that bottom step is frightfully loose,' I warned her, calling down the stair.

Miss Wilhelmina Fickle suddenly poked her head out of the room just opposite. 'Some of us are attempting to teach,' Miss Fickle said sternly, clutching a faded tapestry in her ample hands. 'And would appreciate a little peace and quiet.'

I stepped back and composed myself. 'I am sorry. She's come to me for some guidance. The poor girl is in desperate need of my help,' I said curtly. The enormous Miss Fickle nodded her understanding, then ducked back behind the door.

I returned to my office and watched Mrs McDonald from out of my draughty window as she walked down the street towards Russell Square, parting the crowds as by-standers stepped back to pay homage to her beauty. If only she and I were walking together to the top of Tottenham Court Road, and waiting side by side to catch the Royal Blue Omnibus towards Battersea! How different London would seem – the muddy streets would be lovely, even when crowded with cheapjacks and crossing sweepers, and lined by tinkers and orange girls peddling their wares. The ear-shattering clamour of cartwheels and horse teams would turn to music, and the streams of loose children fighting through the yellow fog would delight us like butterflies as we walked, hand in hand, towards my flat.

I removed myself to my desk and saw that the hastily torn scrap of paper was still folded into the *Gazetteer*. *Release me from my misery*. The words seemed to attack me now, teasing me with some untruth. I castigated myself for letting my imagination get the better of me. I went to my bookshelf and took down one of my father's heavy, leather-bound medical guides, which fell open to the precise passage I knew I needed to read. 'SEXUAL INVERSION: Sexual inversion is a by-product of moral insanity, resulting from congenital reversal of sexual feelings, marked by cerebral anomalies and functional signs of degeneration.'

I quickly pressed the book closed and replaced it on the shelf, feeling the despair rise like a sickness in my throat, as the word 'degeneration' stamped itself behind my eyes and images of Jonnie's body swelled inside my head.

Still, I was determined to help Mrs McDonald. I smiled at the thought of another project to add to my list of good causes. I had fulfilled that particular requirement of woman-hood, even if I had missed most of the others. No one could honestly say that I didn't devote my life to the welfare of my fellow man. Had I not been the winner of the Greater London Societies of Spinsters' 'Generous Helper of the Year' award two years in a row? And was I not the youngest person ever to be elected to the position of a society vice-president, and the third youngest ever to be a regional head?

I had often felt attracted to one of my students, but never to this extent. I could not let it get the better of me. Even so, I could not so easily dismiss the image of Mrs McDonald; the teasing eyelid, the generous lip, the heartfelt request to be released from her misery. Released by me. Why me? What made her suppose I could help? What did I know of husbands?

I felt slightly morose when I returned to my flat in Camberwell that evening. A heaviness hung about my brain, and a quibbling despair touched the edges of my heart, refusing to be dislodged by reminders of the little ways I hoped to change the world. I looked around my flat, anxious to fix on some object that might offer me some comfort. My library was as warm in colour and as richly tobacco-scented as always, filled with my leather armchair, my anatomy diagrams and my rows of calfskin-bound books. My walls were cheered by my collection of picture postcards of musical comedy stars, and a small yellowed skull was still carefully balanced on the shelf. My two matching ginger cats, Happiness and Bliss, seemed as affectionately indifferent to me as ever. But somehow the small trinkets which normally gave me such pleasure seemed shabby and sad.

In the rooms beneath me, deep at the back of the dusty bakery, I could hear the soft cries of the Hambleton children as their mother bathed them and powdered them and rolled them into bed, their soft little bodies as pale and snug as balls of dough. As I unfastened my hair and brushed it, fifty strong strokes with my mother's silver-plated hairbrush, I caught sight of a few grey hairs standing out among the brown. This discovery filled me with unexpected melancholy as I surveyed my bedroom, the vanity top strewn with my beads of jet, my ivory brooches, and my back issues of *The Illustrated London News* carefully marked with articles that warranted reading. Then I considered my sallow face in the oval mirror above me and a dull ache grew up beneath my ribs. 'You have not eaten since morning,' I reminded myself. 'This particular pain should be attributed to nothing more acute than ordinary human hunger.'

I prepared a simple meal of bread, boiled swede, and lentils, and a cup of imported Egyptian cocoa before heading to bed. The book I had been reading was still positioned on the bedside table, next to the tallow candle and the pitcher of cool, coppery-tasting water. I looked at the book's mahogany cover and bright gold leaf, and was tempted to pick it up and dip into the previous night's adventures, which involved shiny brown men wearing falls of flowers and with flowers pressed behind their ears, men who separated breadfruit and coconuts while watching young boys dive from the backs of sharks. My finger slid across the sturdy binding, but I had made a promise, and Tranby Quirke was always good to her word, so instead I settled in with the *1902 Healthy Marriage Guidebook.* A cold draught slipped in around the window, and as I curled the wool cover close to my chin, I could feel the Hambleton children sleeping heavily beneath me. Their breath, in unison, warmed the floor, much as the bakery ovens did in the blackness of each early weekday morning. 'The young would-be mother, with the delicate intention of hoping to conceive', my text began, 'should be free of infection, and spared from any sudden shocks.'

CHAPTER TWO

11 March 1909, a day which seemed to take for ever to arrive, was the wettest day of that particularly storm-tossed spring. The rain came down with such force that the River Thames buckled and broke several bridges, and choked the open docklands, and still the water rose higher and higher, until it was so deep it began to slither, black and oily, through the streets. The Simperton Institute cancelled most of its afternoon classes, and I desperately wished to cancel my meeting with Mrs McDonald. I could not bear to think of her travelling from Hampstead through all that bitter wetness, pressed tight into a closed train carriage, fighting for breath among the umbrellas and overcoats and crying, runny-eyed children and damp, foul-smelling dogs. She was making too much effort to meet me. It was unseemly, as if by meeting in such inauspicious weather, we were agreeing to commit some evil. I had been thinking of her day and night and night and day, and her bright eyes and broad smile hung like grace notes over my everyday activities. 'I will tell her I've been summoned unexpectedly. That's it. Perhaps by my

mentor, Agnes Ellington-Pilch, who has sent word that I am needed immediately . . .' I bargained with myself while I waited apprehensively, desperate to see her, yet equally desperate to flee. And suddenly she appeared before me, knocking confidently on the open doorway, and the rapping of her knuckles shook the wood around my heart.

'Mrs McDonald. I am so pleased to see you again,' I said, welcoming her into the office. The circles under her eyes and the pale cast of her freckled complexion told me she was often sleepless and unwell. 'Do come in and warm yourself.' I helped her remove her overcoat and I worried that my hands were too brusque, and perhaps I was jostling her substantial physique. She was cold and wet, and out of breath from the long trek up the stairs.

'Hello,' she said in a breezy release of breath. 'I've been counting the days until we would meet again.' She handed me the book she had been reading, *Sylvia In Peril On The Peaks Of Ben Nevis*.

'Rather long title,' I commented as I considered the book, which was glossy with raindrops on the cover, and creased where her thumbs had held it intensely. Some of the pages were glued together with moisture, and I thought of how tenderly the book must have rested in her hands and lap, jiggling with the motion of the train.

'Oh, but it's a ripping good read,' she said as she removed her hat and sat down in the wooden chair. A few damp whorls of hair pressed against her face and darkened her porcelain skin, making her appear gaunt and shadowy.

'I've just made some tea. Do have a cup,' I insisted.

'Oh lovely. How thoughtful to have the tea ready just as I arrived,' she said, and her face brightened. Her sweet words sliced a wave of warmth through my internal terra incognita, my untouched middle region.

'Do dry yourself off,' I said as I handed her a lace towel which I had sewn myself on the train to Oxford. She began to dry her face, brushing the soft curls from her ears and neck, but the hair twisted back towards her moist skin, which glowed with renewed life in light of the rubbing. Suddenly the towel looked tattered and obvious, clasped in her hand.

'Thank you, Miss Quirke, that feels much better,' she said, still struggling to catch her breath.

'Oh please, call me Tranby,' I insisted, noticing a tremor in my voice.

'Tranby?' she asked, and I suddenly wished for a more feminine name. I handed her the cup of steaming tea, and as she clasped it, I noticed the cup was chipped at the rim, and I wanted to whisk it away from her, for fear it might puncture her generous lip.

'Yes. Silly name, isn't it?' I poured tea into the other cup, which quivered in my hand.

'No, I like it,' she insisted. As she shook her head the loose curls lapped her neck and shoulders. 'Tran-by. Tran-bee.' She sampled the word, tossing it gingerly on her tongue as if tasting a new and exotic fruit. 'Tranby. It's a very . . . a very definite sort of name. Firm, I'd call it.'

'Really? I always thought it sounded like a village in Cornwall. But I suppose I am used to it now, having struggled with it all my life.'

'How did you come by your name?' she asked, pressing the edge of the chipped cup dangerously close to her lip as her gentle breath disturbed the smooth surface of tea.

'It was the name of my father's best friend. A boyhood chum – Cecil Tranby, killed in the Crimean War. Father had promised to name a son for this dear friend. But Father never had a son. I was the best he could produce. So I was christened Tranby.' I surprised myself. Rarely did I reveal so much to anyone in so short a time. I was astonished at how easily this young woman could open my soul, compelling me to unearth the treasure chest of feelings I had hidden behind my heart, emotions wrapped in tissue and laid aside like precious heirlooms.

Mrs McDonald shuddered a little as she nodded her head. 'They must have been such dear friends for your father to grant his memory such an honour,' she said. The north wind rattled the cracked window and a hissing draught sped through the room. 'Such a sad story, that he died in the war. So young, and he was your father's dear friend.' She lowered her eyes and began to work the edges of her lip. If she began to weep, I was certain to burst open and pour out my soul to her, here and now. I had to change the subject.

'You're from Yorkshire, Mrs McDonald, are you not?' I inquired politely. She blushed and bit her tongue, afraid I'd found something unpleasant in her accent. Nothing could have been further from the truth, for the words she spoke were music.

'Yes. From Easingwold,' she answered shyly. 'And you may call me Lysette, Tranby.'

'Lysette? Is that not French, in origin?' I asked.

'No, not especially. My mother and father are both from Yorkshire as well. They just liked the sound of Lysette, I imagine. Our village was so dull, full of drab Hannahs and Emmas and Marys. I think my parents wanted something that sounded a bit more exotic. Something continental.' She smiled gently, and I noticed she was still shuddering. I could see the outline of dampness around her shoulders. She hadn't told me that she was soaked straight through to the skin.

'Oh dear, Lysette, you're still wet, aren't you? I hadn't realised. Here, let me see if I have a cardigan you can wear. Remove those wet things and we can dry them by the fire.' I motioned her towards me. Dutifully she stood and I helped her take off her bolero jacket, her blouse and her double collar, until only her corset and camisole lay unexplored. Discretion told me to hide my eyes, but something else bade me continue. As I peeled back each layer of clothing she was wetter beneath, and colder, until her thin skin peeped through nearly blue and trembling, and at the sight of this, I began to tremble too. I was so close to her skin that I could smell her expensive perfume, her frequent bathing with lavender soap, a hint of vanilla and a little girlish perspiration.

'Why, you're cold as well,' she remarked, smiling more comfortably and pressing her fingers to the back of my hand. 'I'm glad of it. Oh, not that you're cold, I wouldn't wish that on anyone. No, I'm glad because it means I don't necessarily have sluggish circulation. My grandmother had that, and all her toes turned blue one Christmas.'

I looked into Lysette's bright green eyes and was suddenly seized with the desire to pull her tight to my body and kiss the coldness out of us both. *Resist resist resist*, I said to myself. *Fly death.* I turned away. 'Yes, I am rather cold. Frightfully cold, in fact.' I clasped my arms close to my rattling chest.

I went to the cupboard and took down two thick hand-knit cardigans, handed her one and quickly slid into the other myself. I needed to feel invisible again, to hide beneath protective layers of heavy merino wool. 'This should help us both,' I said. She slipped into the cardigan while I added more coal to the fire and repositioned the fire screen, which I had painted myself with drawings of palm trees and copies of antique maps. I showed her to the settee and she sat down, leaning back and curling into the cardigan while I spread her wet clothing on the back of a chair. Her clothes were expensive, fashionable items that even when damp still kept her shape, memorialising the outline of her beautiful body. I touched the smooth silks and caressed the lace trim and the soft fur collar.

'Oh dear me,' Lysette said sadly, and the shock pierced me like a chill.

'What is it? What's wrong?' I looked up. Lysette had sunk into the centre of the settee. She was weeping gently, and her hair splayed out around her shoulders like a fair silken crown. 'What is it? What's happened, Lysette?'

She sniffled bravely and drew up her shoulders, looking suddenly like the nineteen-year-old girl she truly was. 'I'm ashamed to be seen crying like this,' she said, holding her voice just above the level at which it was certain to break. 'It's not for sadness. It's not for that. I was just thinking how lovely it is to be here in your office. How nice it must be to be you, Tranby Quirke! To teach, to live independently, to have money of your own, to be free to spend and save as you please! What joy it must be to have women friends, to whom you may speak freely of great ideas.'

Oh no, Lysette, no. I am not fit to be your hero. If only you knew. If only you could see the sadness, the loneliness, the lies and the compromises . . .

'I envy you, Tranby. I dreamed all my life of coming to London, and now that I live here, I fear I'll never leave, I'll never break free,' she said, dispelling her last tears with the back of her hand, and brushing her nose roughly with the coarse woollen sleeve.

'But there are always new journeys. No matter where we are at the present moment,' I countered, emphasising the point as I might do in a lecture. 'I need to believe that. If I didn't believe that, I'd be as despairing as Alexander of Macedon, who wept when he felt there were no new worlds left to conquer.'

'Alexander?' she asked, looking puzzled. 'Who's he?'

'Alexander of Macedon. Alexander the Great,' I explained.

'And what did he do that was so wunnnn-derfully great?' she asked.

'What did he do? Why, he was a great soldier. He led his army through Afghanistan to the Indus River; to the eastern limit of the Persian Empire, three hundred and ten years before the time of Christ.'

She scoffed, rolling her eyes. 'Just like a man. Always going off to conquer something or other. Throwing his weight around this way and that. And what of his good lady wife? Tranby, I ask you, what of her? I imagine she had to stay behind in Macedon, minding his babes and having his tea waiting when he got home.' She pursed her full lips, but then softened and smiled wryly. 'Perhaps you should lecture about him sometime this term – I love adventure stories.'

'I would love to lecture about Alexander the Great to my students. Unfortunately . . .' My voice trailed off.

'Unfortunately what?' she asked, leaning forward with great interest as the settee creased beneath her and her tears were quickly forgotten.

'Unfortunately this institution doesn't allow me to teach my girls anything of importance,' I blurted out. 'No, instead we are reduced to teaching trifles like needlework, and floor waxing, and the proper way for a lady to offer a man her dainty, dimpled hands . . .' I stopped suddenly. If Lysette reported my words to the Board of Governors, I could lose my position. I had never been popular with the governors, or indeed with the rest of the staff, particularly the powerful and suspicious Miss Fickle. A sudden silence hung over us uneasily.

Lysette squinted, looking at me from the full depth of her apple-green eyes. 'You're one of the "Votes for Women" ladies, aren't you?'

I would have lied to anyone else. But not to Lysette. 'Yes. I am. I am a member of the Women's Social Political Union, if that's what you mean, and I believe wholeheartedly in the tenets of the suffragist campaign.' She raised one thin blond eyebrow at me, but said nothing. 'Don't you believe women should vote, Mrs McDonald?'

She burst out laughing with such freedom and such vigour that her chest shook and small lines danced around her almond-shaped eyes. 'Of course I do. But what does that matter? Even if other women may vote, I shall never be able to. Malcolm wouldn't allow it. It's a man's world, Miss Quirke, no matter how you cut it up.'

'But surely the—'

She interrupted before I could finish. 'Men make rules for other men. Men make men's laws. So women can vote? That means nothing but that women can choose one man or another, to make the same men's rules.' She spoke passionately, not bothering to hide her accent. No student had ever addressed me with such impudence, and I had reprimanded girls for lesser transgressions than this. But instead of being angry, I was refreshed by her honesty. 'So I reckon I'll never make your list of female achievers, Miss Quirke,' she added deftly.

'Oh please, do call me Tranby,' I said, regaining my composure. 'And as I've explained in class, a female achiever is any woman who contributes something of value to the world. You may still become an achiever, Lysette. I for one have not yet counted you out.' Lysette smiled again, relaxing back in the settee as if the revelation of my secret suffragette tendencies had drawn us closer together.

'A female achiever. Malcolm wouldn't allow that either,' she said sarcastically, folding her arms.

'Have you been married long, Lysette?' I asked. She was silent for a moment, pursing her full lips with such force they began to turn white. 'Too long. A year and a half. Far too long. But what else could I do? I was sent to work as a dairy maid at Ogleton Manor when I was thirteen years old. You see, I have five brothers, so I was the one mouth too many. I worked at Ogleton Manor for four years, until the day Malcolm McDonald came to visit. He's a commercial traveller you see, and when Malcolm saw me in the scullery he fell in love with me at that very instant. That very instant, I tell you, Tranby! Malcolm spoke to my father, and they both agreed that I should marry him and move to London to be his partner, helpmate, and wife.' Her mouth twisted into a sad little smile. 'Just like in a romance novel,' she whispered bitterly.

'Does it not concern you that you were given away as part of a business deal, the sort of arrangement men might make over cattle? Does it not bother you that you were treated as something less than human?' I asked her pointedly as my own skin grew dry and tight from the heat of the fire.

She looked at me a long moment then shrugged her shoulders. 'Treated like something less than a man, you mean. Not less than human, less than a man. Well, what can I say? At least they asked me if I wanted to marry him. At least they asked me. Some girls don't even get that.' She sighed. 'Of course I said yes to the marriage. I would have said yes to anything to get me away from Ogleton Manor and away from Master Harry, he with his bull whips and his bridle and his candles, and his oily cheeks and his dirty fingernails . . .'

My heart stirred at the thought of her struggles. I had underestimated her, mistakenly assuming that her beauty had spared her from sorrow. 'Oh, Lysette, I am truly sorry to hear this.' I moved closer to her, in fact I was about to offer her a firm pat on the shoulder, but she stopped me in my steps.

'Don't be sorry. I don't need sympathy. I need to know how to join the pudding club.'

I slid back behind my desk and resumed the manner of a lecturer. 'Very well then, Lysette. Unfortunately, there is not much I can offer for advice.' I picked up my notes. 'First of all, you must indulge your husband.' The words caught like a sharp bone in my throat. 'Whenever and wherever your husband requests it, you must, above all, must comply. It is a fact that men need to release themselves physically. A man can become ill, even sterile or insane, if he withholds himself too long. Your regular and natural coupling with your husband should, in time, result in pregnancy. In the meantime, you should endeavour to eat plenty of bread, but avoid butter and drippings. Take no hot drinks right before bedtime . . . Try to avoid episodes of social excitement.' I recited the facts plainly, without much expression, and she closed her eyes, lost in the softness of the settee and the warmth of the fire. She nodded occasionally, so I would know she was still listening.

'I love the sound of your voice. I could listen to you for ages,' she said dreamily, eyes closed and face reflecting the fire's russet-coloured light.

My voice? Suddenly I had no voice. No one had ever loved my voice. A cackle emerged from my throat as I tried to speak again. 'The duty of the young mother is to uphold the purity of the English race . . . The recent and troubling increase in infant mortality can be directly traced to ignorant women and neglectful mothering . . .' I continued with this nonsense. I knew I had to keep speaking, for fear she might start suddenly and in the silence hear my heart pounding and realise how transfixed I was, watching the firelight sizzle and dance off her golden blond hair. *Come home with me, Lysette. Follow me back to the little flat in Camberwell. Remove your wet garments and lie by my fire, let us wrap our arms around each other and stay quiet, side by side throughout the night . . .* The dream flowed through my head, passing like a silent stream beneath my empty words.

'Lysette, it is now ten minutes before five,' I told her loudly. The fire had burned down without my noticing it, and now my office was soft and smoky, darkly laced with a vegetable smell. 'Lysette,' I said again. I didn't trust my hands if I dared to touch her shoulder. 'Your train will be leaving soon.' Her eyes, as they opened, were slightly swollen, and a red cleft marked the side of her cheek, where her face had rested heavily against her hand. Even so, she was no less beautiful than the moment she had walked in. Her eyes took on a far-away expression as she smiled at me and struggled to get up. 'Oh, Tranby, I was imagining something lovely,' she confided. As she rose I gave her a mixture of herbs which I had had the chemist specially prepare.

'I'm certain this will help,' she said, with a note of forced optimism as she grabbed the packet and stuffed it into her handbag. She slipped off the cardigan and I helped her back into her clothes, which were dry now, but stiff and stubborn from resting on the chair. She pulled them on roughly, jamming her arms through the sleeves and struggling with the buttons.

'When shall we meet again?' she asked, brushing against my arm and letting her hand rest contentedly on my elbow. 'I fear I shall need quite a bit more of your help.' For a moment she reminded me of Jonnie, the spark in her eyes, the broad smile.

'I . . . I'm n-not certain,' I stuttered.

'But don't you want to see me?' she asked, stiffening slightly.

'Of course I do. It's just that, well, I've been quite busy recently, and my spare time is very precious. And I do have other students to consider, who often need my help and advice.'

I watched the hurt echo through her eyes and resonate deep in her features before she caught hold of herself and straightened her face. 'Of course you do. How selfish of me not to consider your other students. You've been so helpful. Thank you so much for everything.'

Suddenly I could not bear to see her leave my office on a note of such unhappiness. 'Lysette, I'm certain you will be expecting a child one day very soon. I will wish for it during my evening meditations.' I tried to sound cheerful.

'Of course,' she said, rubbing her bleary eyes. 'Thank you again.' I showed her to the door and she left my office, pausing long enough to wave a grave good-bye. This time I did not lead her to the staircase, but I did watch from my window as she hurried down the street, struggling to prevent her overcoat from flying off her shoulders.

I should have roused her earlier, I chided myself. She was walking unevenly, one hand holding her hat to her head and the other hand on her abdomen as she dodged the pelting raindrops and the cloth-capped urchins streaming down the street. She shifted from toe to bootheel to toe again, and I worried that the shaking of her insides might make her ill. I routinely ministered to the sick through my work with The Society, in fact I was an occasional companion to my mentor, the famed suffragist Agnes Ellington-Pilch, but even so, the ill and infirm always inspired in me feelings of gnawing impatience and a dull superiority. But if Lysette were ill, I would stand beside her sickbed, grateful for the chance to hold her hand . . .

No. No. I knew I could not afford to entertain such dangerous ideas. I moved across my office and stoked the fire until the flames nearly leapt into the room, but even in that heat a chill clung to my insides, thickening like frost between my bones and sealing off the last passages of my lungs. I sat down to read my students' reports and finish my weekly bookkeeping, but the same persistent ache which I had felt throughout that spring seemed again to be tapping at the backs of my ribs, and my hands shook with such tremors I was forced to clasp them in my lap.

Suddenly I stepped over to the crumpled cardigan, and in a show of reckless abandon, pressed it to my face. I wanted to disappear into it, I wanted to extract Lysette's essence from the fibre of the wool itself. The feeling frightened me. I had so much to lose, if I were foolish. The very world seemed tipped, ready to unravel.

After much deep breathing, I took a swig of sweet madeira wine which I kept in my office for purely medicinal purposes, and a dose of hartshorn from my small glass smelling bottle. I recalled my father's advice that listing one's troubles was the best way to end them. On a sheet of crisp letterhead stationery I wrote out the nature of my dilemma. I reminded myself of my duty as an instructor of young women to set the proper social tone, to drive the moral high road at all times. I played physician to myself, and attempted to reduce to ordered terms this unsettling development.

DIAGNOSIS: Love.
No. Not possible.
SYMPTOMS: Giddiness, shortness of breath. Urge to gather flowers. No. Lips that long to kiss. No. No. Tremors in hands and knees. Flightiness and his twin pain, optimism. General soreness in thorax. Rash on neck. No. Soft tissue breaks out in hives, in the pattern of the rose bush raising thorns. NO. My heart hurts. Poked and nibbled by plush, carnation-flavoured lips. NO!
PROGNOSIS: Poor.
ANTIDOTE: Lysette. A last desperate bid to live: Lysette.

CURE: Unknown to man. Lysette McDonald. Yes. Only Lysette. Lysette Lysette Lysette.

I tore up the note as quickly as I wrote it, then threw the pieces into the fire and watched them sizzle and squeal until I was certain every shred of evidence had turned to ash. I could see I would need much more madeira, and as an extra precautionary measure, I prepared some lemon balm. I caught hold of my senses and reassembled my thoughts. Then I wrote this note: *Mrs McDonald, Thank you for meeting with me on Tuesday afternoon. Your future attendance in my class is secure. Miss T. Quirke.*

CHAPTER THREE

I returned to my flat that evening intending to work on my report regarding the spread of the Gospel in the Belgian Congo, but the rains which had fallen all day scarcely abated before returning, dark and menacing and blustery. The roof rattled, the windows shook and the cats stalked the perimeter of the room in terror. Bliss's mournful miaowing punctuated the silence between thunder bolts, his mouth like a tiny pink gash opening in his frightened orange face. I tried to comfort him, but just as I cradled him close to my chin, a crash of lightning split the sky. He jumped from my arms, scurrying beneath the bed. I felt a scratch on my neck prickle with thin blood and sadness swelled inside me. Even the cat suffered my love.

My mind wandered and I couldn't concentrate. When I had been afraid of storms as a child, Father would sit beside me and patiently explain about the force of clouds colliding, the pressure of the air, the moisture rising from and returning to the earth, and the science made sense, or at least I pretended it did, because his voice was comfort enough. Where was Lysette? I suddenly wondered. What was she doing now? Lying bereft in her marriage bed, most likely. I tried not to think of her, shivering beneath the blanket, hiding her silvery tears from the gaze of her indifferent husband. Where was Jonnie? Buried on a lonely hill somewhere, quiet and deep beneath the ground.

The night was too dark, too lonely, too loud, and all the warm cocoa in the world would not send me to sleep. There was only one escape from this sort of despair. I lit my spiced candle, took my black-covered book from its box beneath the bed, filled my pen with ink and sat down to a session of automatic writing.

I began with a series of deep breathing exercises to clear my head and block out the roar of the storm. I had neglected to draw the curtain and suddenly a crack of lightning illuminated my reflection in the window. The image frightened me. My face was like a skull, so dark and hollow, and my body was ghostly as well, draped in a simple white nightdress with my hair tucked up under a cap. But that wasn't me; that didn't need to be me. I, yes I, could be free. I relaxed and let my spirit soar, filling the empty vessel of my body with the thrill of other lives and other worlds.

My darling Lysette – Let this midnight meditation be your message, let me tell you how far I'll travel to embrace your love. All the words forbidden on my tongue in daylight, let them spring to life at night, when safe and silent beneath the bedsheets, my mind, released, takes flight.

I have passed the fifteen-hundredth mile of the Great Wall of China. I am in the entourage of Marco Polo, travelling on a golden passport in the name of the great Kublai Khan. I am a man now. Or at least, I am no longer woman. We cover 70-odd miles every day, and sleep standing up, using our bodies and our horses as a shield against the windstorms, and this prevents me from spending any time investigating my gender. And anyway, it does not matter here, so long as I am tough and strong and quiet, and the other men nod to me, grunt out loud and hand me the leather pouch of brackish water, and do not mind when I hold it to my withered lips.

We are returning to Venice after 13 years of exile, and scarcely can I believe the dangers I have braved. I have marched beside bands of wild Tartars who stopped only long enough to slit their horses' breasts and drink the blood. I have stepped foot inside the great Khan's court, with his pools of waterfowl and gleaming goldfish, and seen the blossoming trees which he commands never to lose their leaves, and these same trees, out of honour or out of fearfulness, dare not disobey him. I have been a guest in Kinsai, the secret city of Heaven, where the palaces are large enough to hold 100 feasts in 100 different halls, all at the very same hour, with enough servants on hand to serve ten to a guest. I have drunk strange liquors outside arched pagodas whose pointed roofs were the colour of fresh-cut cinnamon, and I have parted bamboo curtains and gazed on royal dark-eyed concubines eagerly inviting me to join them in their feast. I have found refuge in the oasis town of Kashgar, where I paused long enough to drink restorative waters while surrounded by smiling Buddhas, before resuming my journey on the perfumed rivers and roads of silk.

And through all these travels I have never, for an instant, stopped longing for you, Lysette, even as I gazed into the demonic eyes of court sorcerers who madly spun dishes and filled dancing cups. I thought of you as I watched a golden temple rise suddenly from dust, and when I threw light into a darkened ruby mine, and saw my face reflected on blood-red walls, and when I stood in the shadow of an oil fountain gushing so high and so black it blotted out the sun. I asked for your blessing before I bit into the broiled flesh of exotic game birds, and prayed for your deliverance as I battled ferocious porcupines and wild, red-eyed dogs. But still I have not found the courage to love you. I did not find it among the jade, the red clay, or the delicate porcelain, nor within the caves of Tibetan musk; and not among the white pears beneath the tails of golden partridges.

I have searched for that courage on the Roof of the World, the 12,000-foot peaks where the mountains stretch higher and higher in ranges so lofty no birds have wings or lungs enough to reach the summit, and fire is a lesser force, too weak to boil water. Here men become breathless simply by standing, or by too-swiftly turning their heads, so I descended into Sinkiang, a verdant, mild region of amber-leaved trees, delicately fragrant breezes, and riverbeds rich with chalcedony and jasper.

This morning we reached the Takla Makan Desert, famous for its singing sands and feverish mirages. The entourage will stop here for a while, taking time to rest our horses, bandage our burnt yellow feet, cover our heads and keep our arms safe from the sun. The friendly Tartars warned us about the desert's strange voices, which sing so sweetly that they lure travellers to their deaths, filling the air with the music of tuned instruments and the metallic clash of fighting arms, tempting soldiers to sleepwalk to their deaths.

As I write these words, some men are sleeping, open-mouthed and on their backs, and others talk softly, smoking clay pipes or dipping into pouches of preserved meat.

Others stretch and sigh and loosen their outer garments which are heavy with stolen diamonds sewed into re-inforced seams; clothes that stand upright even when empty. I walk away from the quiet camp, scattering the sand with my feet. The other men think me odd, but they are not suspicious. These men believe that I'm homesick, and pining for a woman, and of course they are correct, and here and now there is nothing unusual about that fact. 'Quer-ke,' they call me, 'Quer-ke,' to get my attention as they mimic me. They sigh and they swoon, stage elaborate pratfalls into each others arms, pucker their lips and flutter their hands above their hearts, teasing me for being in love; and although I brush away these comments, deep within my empty innards I am thrilled. This is the most public love I have ever known, even though you are thousands of miles, and thousands of years, away from me now.

Lysette, how I long for you here, but I dare not indulge this weakness, this feminine weakness, this urge to release myself through tears, even though I have seen brave men cry for less than this; for a lost horse, for an opened blister, for a last drink of water. I am thirsty now too, but only for the liquid of your kisses. I am lost inside myself, lost in the desert without your life-giving love.

PART TWO

'Women are angels, wooing . . .'

Troilus and Cressida

CHAPTER FOUR

Following our meeting of 11 March, I vowed never to speak privately with Lysette McDonald again. My midnight writing frightened me, made me fear I was losing my grasp of the everyday world. The very thought of Lysette burnt furrows in my careful life, and her winks and her smiles were like little acid arrows that bit into the softness of my heart.

Meanwhile the rains ended and spring advanced, along with the phantom pains that spread from my chest into my limbs, filling me with a melancholy so distracting that I barely noticed the freshening breezes or the greening of the trees. I kept myself busy correcting students' papers, devising advertisements for a firm of cabinet makers, and labouring over five-sovereign contest prizes as offered in the weekly newspapers.

My work with The British Society For The Aid Of Distressed Spinsters And Gentlewomen-In-Need grew much more involving. By the beginning of April it had become imperative that we find the funds to build our proposed nursing home in Notting Hill, due to the quickly deteriorating physical condition of

Agnes Ellington-Pilch, the society's patron and founder, and my own personal mentor. She was ill with quinsy and rheumatism, and the doctors had said her weakened heart would only survive another few months. I had volunteered to care for her twice a week, travelling to Belgravia on Wednesday and Friday evenings to feed her porridge oats and read to her from the collected poems of Tennyson and the essays of Beatrice Webb.

Please. I need to see you again. Please don't tell me no. A hot flush rose to my cheeks as I read the note hastily pressed into my fist. No signature was needed. I knew the letter came from Lysette, and I could feel her desperation as it spread from the scrap of paper, through my skin and into my blood. Her eyes, clear and full of hope, called out to me across the classroom, begging for attention.

My reply was polite and to the point, and I had the messenger girl deliver it to Lysette that afternoon. *I'm sorry I will not be able to meet with you. Unfortunately, previous engagements will prevent me from holding office hours this week. Pray forgive me, T. Quirke.*

Two days later Lysette stopped me in the corridor of the Simperton Institute. There was a daily ten-minute break in the lecture, during which the girls powdered their noses, or blotted their foreheads of the excess oils brought forth by the strains of serious study.

'Please, Tranby, I must see you. I need to talk to you about something extremely important,' Lysette pleaded, pushing me against a doorway and clinging intensely to my arm. She looked lovely, dressed in a velvet frock of bittersweet brown, cinched tight at the waist and falling in loose pleats that swept to the floor. Her hair was piled high atop her head with a few tendrils dripping deliciously down to her ears. 'Please?' she asked again.

I noticed how close we were to the classroom of Miss Fickle, and I couldn't ignore the fearful tapping of boot pattens as numerous students milled about the hallways. Anyone could see us, and might wonder what business could cause us to speak so quietly and to stand so close.

'Mrs McDonald, I would like to help you, certainly. But I am very busy at present and I simply do not have a moment to spare,' I insisted.

'Why won't you meet with me? Why do I seem to frighten you so?' she asked, squeezing my arm. How I wished I could tell her of my fear, that any affection squeezed out of me would be the end of us both.

'This is neither the time nor the place to discuss these matters,' I whispered fiercely. The rush of my breath disturbed the soft hair on her forehead.

She looked deep into my eyes. 'Well, perhaps in a few weeks' time? Would I be able to see you then?' she asked, undaunted.

'Yes. That might be acceptable,' I said evenly.

Her hand loosened on my arm. She smiled. 'I knew you would not disappoint me. That much was certain,' she said, slipping away from me and dipping unnoticed into the crowd of gabbling girls.

That evening when I made my regular visit to Belgravia, I found Agnes in an unusually pensive mood. No doubt her illnesses were troubling her, and the increasing infirmity must have been difficult for such a strong-willed and independent woman. But something had changed; a tremor shook her hand, a rheumy liquid filled her eyes. Agnes was normally scrupulous in her presentation, but tonight her hair was wiry and her clothing askew. Even Hotspur, her terrier, seemed out of sorts as he paced the floor, whimpering and pretending to dig. I was struck by the thought that I was looking at someone who knew she was going to die, then I chided myself for such a morbid and uncharitable thought. Of course she isn't going to die, I told myself.

'I've brought you some oranges,' I said to Agnes, thinking my little gift might lift her spirits. I sat down at the table and made a small show of gestures to get her attention, setting out a blue Delft plate, a sharp-edged knife, and a fine lace serviette. I took an orange in my hand and broke the tough fragrant skin, smelling the sweet juices and carving up the segments, arranging them on the plate with delicate attention to detail.

'Thank you, Tranby,' Agnes said. 'I think I'll have that later, if you don't mind.' She pushed the plate away.

'Very well,' I said, respecting her wishes. I hoped nothing was wrong. Perhaps she'd had bad news. I wanted to ask her, but I couldn't bring myself to be so familiar. Agnes and I had a strange relationship. Clearly, she liked me and respected my work; indeed, she had chosen me as her successor over several other society members. I knew by her comments that she considered my intelligence far superior to other women's, and she admired the fact that I disdained the vanities of femininity and never regretted not having had children. Yet Agnes was a severe and impatient woman, impossible to please. I never felt I could laugh or smile easily in her presence, and I often felt when she looked at me with her steely eyes that she weighed and measured me, and found me lacking in some significant feature.

I covered the orange slices with the serviette and took up the book of Tennyson poems. 'Shall I begin with "The Charge of the Light Brigade"?' I asked, knowing it was her favourite. Her eyelids dropped slowly, a slight gesture which I interpreted as a nod. Her hands shook as she pulled the blanket over her shoulders. I cleared my throat and began to read. I always hated the way my voice broke on a silent room, but usually, once I settled into a rhythm, I found a pleasant echo in the gentle swell of syllables and pauses. 'Half a league, half a league, Half a league onward, All in the valley of Death, Rode the six hundred,' I began.

It was a dry, still night, the first quiet night in ages, and the silence without emphasised every murmur within. When I paused for breath I could hear the flutter of a candle, the tick of the clock on the mantelpiece, and the scratch of a squirrel or rat on the roof.

'Forward, the Light Brigade . . .'

'No, Tranby, please, read it with more feeling!' Agnes suddenly commanded. 'You're sending them to their deaths as if they've just popped out for a cup of tea.'

'Sorry,' I murmured, surprised by her outburst. I cleared my throat and began again, this time aware of how weak and nasal my vowels sounded. 'Forward, the Light Brigade! Charge for the guns! he said: Into the valley of Death, Rode the six hundred.'

'Rode the six hundred!' she repeated, in a firm voice which surprised me with its youthful vigour. I looked up and she had her fist held up before her face, and her liquidy eyes were suddenly fiery with defiance. The image nearly made me laugh aloud, and yet seemed in the next instant to be almost unbearably poignant.

'You recite so much better than I,' I said tentatively. 'Perhaps we should read it together?'

She let out a deep breath and her hand slipped to her lap. She seemed deflated, as if all her energy had gone into the recitation of one energetic line. 'No, I think not. Read something gentler. I would like to hear, "In Memoriam".'

Dutifully I turned the pages. I had serious misgivings about delving into something so melancholic, but I didn't dare defy her wishes. I cleared my dry throat and began to read. 'Dark house, by which once more I stand, Here in the long unlovely street, Doors, where my heart was used to beat, So quickly, waiting for a hand . . .'

'Tranby, could you not read it with a bit more feeling?' she interrupted, rocking back in her chair. The forced politeness in her voice made the rebuke sound all the sharper. 'There is so much passion there, so much sorrow in the verse. Feel the sadness of the poet's loss. The reader has a duty to bring that feeling to life.'

I felt myself blush and my throat narrowed still further. 'Shall I begin again?'

'Yes, if you wouldn't mind.'

'Dark house, by which once more I stand, Here in the long unlovely street, Doors, where my heart was used to beat, So quickly, waiting for a hand . . .' I glanced up and saw her face, firmly set and tightly lined. I stumbled, lost my place, then started again, determined to invoke more feeling. '. . . Doors, where my heart was used to beat . . .' Shame rose up my neck as I saw her shaking her head, clearly pained by my reading. It must be terrible, I told myself. I longed to stop, but could not bear the thought of enduring an embarrassed silence. I wished to jump up and run out of the house, fleeing the uneasiness and instead embrace the cool evening air. I wanted to run as far and as fast as I could from age, illness, and death. But I knew I had a duty to stay at Agnes' side. 'A hand that can be clasp'd no more – Behold me, for I cannot sleep, And like a guilty thing I creep, At earliest morning to the door.'

As I read further, I stole occasional furtive glances between stanzas, and saw that her face had settled. Her eyes were closed and her head nodded in rhythm with the words.

Perhaps I'm not so bad after all, I told myself. Perhaps I am improving. I read on and on, my voice strengthening with each line and the familiar words carving themselves into my mind with new intensity.

'Be near me when my light is low, When the blood creeps, and the nerves prick And tingle; and the heart is sick, And all the wheels of Being slow.' The last line got caught in my chest and I could barely breathe it out. The words disturbed me as an unpleasant odour spread through the room and a gripping chill inched up from the floor. I looked towards Agnes and was shocked to see she was weeping. A few cold, silent tears moved evenly down her cheeks. Her fist, the one she had raised so defiantly in the service of the Light Brigade, was now pressed tightly to her breast. It was not a gesture of pain, but one of determination, determination not to let that weak heart cease its beating. Hotspur had climbed into her lap and she stroked his head intently. He looked up at her, licking her hand with his pale pink tongue. His weak back legs were trembling and his wiry grey muzzle was stained dark yellow, but his patient brown eyes appeared inexplicably full of love. The bad odour emanated from him, but he seemed to be suitably embarrassed by it, and Agnes clearly was not repelled. She stroked him over and over and he sat patiently, the two of them locked in a quiet communion of age and infirmity. I thought perhaps I should say something to Agnes, but instead I turned away. Her sorrow, whatever its source, was controllable, and it was something too private for me, too large and foreboding. It was a solemn room I was forbidden to enter. I took up again with reading.

'Be near me when I fade away, To point the term of human strife, And on the low dark verge of life, The twilight of eternal day . . .'

*

'That was fine, thank you,' Agnes said easily when the poem was ended. It is so good of you to care for me.' Her tears had dried and Hotspur slept peacefully, his chin resting on her knee, her hands cupped protectively under his belly. Whatever sadness had gripped her had now passed away, and all that remained was a cool, dark, comfortable evening. I felt relieved and at ease.

I helped Agnes wash and dress for bed, and a quiet under-standing seemed to pass between our bodies. I folded down the bedsheets and smoothed away the wrinkles, tucking her safely beneath the blanket. 'Now, remember to let Hotspur out, and then wipe his feet with the cloth when he comes in again,' she instructed. Her mind struggled to stay awake while her body gave in to sleeping. 'Gather up those notes which I left on the table, I'll need those for the meeting on Thursday. Put out the empty milk churn and . . .' Her features looked soft and smooth in the candlelight, and I could imag-ine her thirty years younger, with jet-black hair; wise, vibrant, hazel-coloured eyes, and an intellect that could match any man. Leaning over her to straighten her nightcap, I had the strange urge to kiss her. I wanted to plant my lips on her elderly forehead, and immediately I thought this, I felt myself blush. Why such sudden and wanton tenderness for an elderly associate? There was a connection to Lysette, I was certain. She had made me gentler, she had opened my heart to new things. Made me aware of more softness in the world. Thinking of Lysette and the youthful freshness of her lips took away my desire to kiss Agnes, which was probably just as well, for I imagined it would have disturbed her immensely, had she woken in the dark and felt the pressure of my lips against her skin. I thought I might weep, something sharp caught in the corner of my eye, but I swallowed hard and the feeling retreated. Agnes had made me her successor, which was a great honour, but also gave me much to live up to. I had to learn to be steadfast and firm with my emotions, to measure out my tears, and spend them only when necessary.

I blew out the candle and went downstairs. I heard the floorboards creaking as Agnes settled into the bed. I gathered up the oranges, stacked the teacups and put away her books. I was aware of how quiet I was, as if I were respecting some request for silence, or had dressed myself in sworn solemnity. I've done a good deed this evening, I told myself as I closed and locked the door. I stayed beside Agnes in her moment of doubt, and when she recovered, all was well between us. I returned home contemplating Agnes' world of neatness and order, her manner of old age which I aspired to, and my own hope of someday having her same confidence of a job well done.

CHAPTER FIVE

By the middle of April, Lysette's attendance at my class had
became irregular. She was absent as many days as she was
present, although never, not for a moment, was she absent
from my thoughts. I agonised that I was at fault, that my
refusal to see her had hurt her deeply, or worse, that my desire
had become a visible thing. I feared I might be frightening her
away with the hidden pulse of my longing. Her marks, which
had never been top of the class, began to drop. When she did
attend class, resplendent in silk hats and ivory cameos, she
often looked pale and sickly, and even her full lips seemed to
be fading, gradually losing colour.

When she was present, sitting in the second row, third from
the left, her beauty teased me as a powerful distraction. I lived
in a gentle hell; nervous each moment, but basking in Lysette's
attention. I glowed in the joy of knowing that for an hour, I
starred on her stage. I thrilled to see the workings of her brain
revealed in her features. I watched the light in her eyes as her
forehead furrowed, then opened, and I imagined her body
beneath, just as alive. And yet I kept myself constantly in

check. Whenever I felt myself losing control over my lecture, I inwardly recited several important Simperton tenets: *Upright carriage equals upright character; moral backbone, moral mind; steady step and steady head; clear eyes and clean thoughts; discipline, discipline, discipline.*

On the day that I returned Lysette's written report on the proper procedures for storing cooking fats, I saw the faint shadow of bruises on her arm, in the small space of freckled skin between her glove and folded velvet cuff. I gasped, then recovered myself. Images of Jonnie's body floated to the top of my mind, like an augury of what would happen if I dared to pursue her love. On the other hand, it was clear to me that Lysette's husband continued to beat her, perhaps more fervently than before. I decided to intervene. Lysette was my student, and helping a student was as much my responsibility as lecturing or marking papers.

When I returned Lysette's assignment on the proper procedure for addressing envelopes intended for one's social betters, I attached this note to the top: *Mrs McDonald, I'm sorry to inform you that I must ask you to return to my office at once. A matter raised at our previous meeting unfortunately has not been settled to my satisfaction. Would you be so good as to meet me on the 17th of April promptly at half four in my office at the Simperton Institute? Yours, T.Q.*

I sat back and watched her as she read the note once, then read it again and let the words play silently across her lips. She looked up at me, beaming. Her eyes glowed gratefully, and I watched her mouth the words, 'Thank you, thank you, thank you,' over and over. Then she puckered her lips and bestowed on me an imaginary kiss.

My darling Lysette – My search for courage continues. The

year is 1498, and I am travelling with Vasco da Gama, heading towards Calicut on India's Malabar Coast. My love for you, so hidden in my home life, has emboldened me by night. As recently as yesterday, I led the troops along the route to meet the tall Zamorin, the tan-skinned Hindu king, whom we found lounging nonchalantly on three thick cushions atop a green velvet couch. The king, in greeting, offered da Gama a banana, but da Gama, fearing poison, declined. Let history remember I was the first Westerner brave enough to taste the fleshy yellow fruit and declare it safe, tasty, and delicious. Tomorrow I will lead the march through forests thick with ebony, sandal-wood, and teak, and I promise that once I reach the ocean, I will find you and we will sneak away together, deep into the fields, and make love amid the pepper and the ginger-root, the cardamom and cloves, and afterwards, as we lie wrapped within each other's arms, the low-hung air will be so heavy and so fragrant that it will be difficult to sleep, and impossible to dream of anything but feasting.

On 15 April, Wilhelmina Fickle rushed to my office, red-faced and puffing, saying that Mrs McDonald was downstairs and wished to see me. Her announcement caught me off-guard. I checked my calendar again – it was indeed 15 April, and I was not expecting Lysette for another two days.

'I wasn't aware that you had any appointments scheduled this morning . . .' Miss Fickle began.

'No, it's quite all right,' I answered quickly. 'I can find a few minutes to spare.'

'Knowing how busy you are, I suggested she return later and enquire . . .'

'No. Please, send her upstairs at once!' I interrupted.

'As you wish,' she said, turning on her heels.

My lip began to tremble and I desperately needed my smelling bottle. I wished to drink a flagon of madeira, and top it off with a deep swig of gin. Lysette was on her way to meet with me again, and I felt terribly unprepared. If she so much as smiled at me, I would have no choice but to send her home at once.

I heard the anxious tapping clatter of Lysette's bootheels as she hurried towards my office, and the insistent rhythm echoed the throbbing in my skull. 'Miss Quirke, I mean Tranby, something horrible has happened,' she said as she stepped into my office. My thoughts were racing as obscene images rose in my mind like soured cream to the top of strong coffee, words and worse, their attendant images of rape and wounds and knives and violation, and I could hardly get the words out of my mouth.

'What is it, Lysette, what is it?' I wanted to fold her into my arms, safe and warm. 'Please, tell me what has happened.'

'My husband,' she stuttered, dipping into the wooden chair, 'he wants me to leave your course on *Popular Thought for Modern Women*. He says book-learning is bad for women, gives them too many notions, and he thinks you've spoilt me.' She slipped her white handkerchief from her handbag and began to turn it over and over, tightening in her hand.

I was stunned. Spoiled? I thought about a gift opened early, or a surprise too soon revealed, or perhaps like a fruit left on the vine too long and spoiled by the sun. How could I have *spoiled* anything?

'Malcolm and I had a quarrel this morning, and he says book-learning makes me less good-looking. He says I've been thinking too much, and it's wrinkling my forehead.' She spat out the words defiantly.

'I'm sorry, Lysette, truly sorry. Your husband sounds like a dreadful man,' I responded.

She bit her lip impatiently. 'He slapped me when he found me reading a suffragism pamphlet. I thought I had it well hidden, but he searches through all my things. Malcolm says, and these are his very words, "Why should a woman want to vote? What has been decided among the prehistoric protozoa cannot be changed by an act of Parliament."'

'I've heard that comment several times myself. Have you tried to indulge your husband? Have you made an honest effort to understand and satisfy his needs?' I asked, disgusted by the thought of what I was suggesting.

'It's no use,' she insisted. 'My situation is getting worse and worse.'

'Do you mean to say he beats you more frequently?' I asked, quaking at the image of her body battered and bruised and face down in a stream.

'No. That is not the problem. He still beats me, but I could accept that. I expect most men beat their wives. No, Tranby, my problem is something far worse.'

'What is it, Lysette? Please, confide in me. I am your instructor. You can trust me with anything.'

'Indeed, I believe I can.' She pulled the handkerchief tighter between her fists and steadied herself in the chair. Then she took a breath so deep I could see the muscles struggling in her throat. 'I've begun to desire women. In the Biblical sense of desire, if you know what I mean,' she said, pressing her hand to her chest.

I was stunned. I felt as if I had been born again, for an instant. The world was suddenly full of new possibilities. If Lysette could love women, she could love me. Was it possible? *But slow down, old girl*, I warned myself. There are thousands of women in London alone. *Why would she love you?*

'Well, Lysette, this is an interesting development,' I said following a brief pause. My words were firm, but in my head, a high-pitched voice screamed out at her: *Save it. Keep it. Be true to yourself. Yes, Lysette, love women. Yes. Love them. Jump into it with your whole being. Be brave in the ways I haven't been.*

'You must be so disappointed,' she said carefully, removing her hat, setting it down beside her and gauging my face for some reaction. 'Did you ever imagine I might prove to be so strange? Now I'm for ever out of reach of the ranks of the female achievers.'

I was touched by the poignancy of the thought that this was something that actually mattered to her. She twisted the cambric handkerchief tight between her fingers, until the whiteness of her knuckles showed through her net gloves, and her teeth, pulling the edges of her lips, had brought them to the verge of bleeding. Love was all but bursting from me by this time. *Tell, Tranby, tell, reveal what has been hidden.* The pressure was immense.

'Oh, Lysette, you aren't strange. Many people have these feelings, people who are otherwise quite "ordinary".' I looked at her, feigning an expression of pity and detachment.

'Do you really think so?' she asked.

'Of course,' I answered as I moved closer to her chair. I offered her a dish of arrowroot biscuits and she eagerly grabbed one and pushed it into her mouth.

'I'm so glad you understand. I knew I could turn to you, you and no one else. You do understand,' she said, as she broke into tears. Her fingers crumbled another biscuit and tightened on the handkerchief as her fist rubbed the tears deep into her puffy eyes.

I gently caressed her shoulder, frightened of how close she was to me, and how easy it would be to give into my deepest feelings. 'Oh, Lysette, don't weep. All may yet be well,' I said, as something possessed me to kiss the shining top of her head, where the hair parted on a knife-line and fell in amber ringlets. She looked up at me and tried to smile, drawing the loose tears and the biscuit crumbs back into her throat.

'It is such a relief to know I am not alone. At last we can be honest with one another,' she said, embracing me warmly and pressing her forehead against my chest.

I pulled away. 'What are you suggesting?' I asked as a spasm of fear closed my throat, and I thought about the possibility of Miss Fickle looking in on us at any moment.

Lysette's tear-pinched eyes narrowed. 'You understand, surely. You are yourself, are you not . . .'

'No,' I interrupted her. 'No. No. No.' Freeing myself from her arms I stepped quickly back behind my desk. 'Lysette, this is a complicated issue. Women can not simply . . .'

'But we could! Let's run away together, Tranby,' she said.

'And where would we go? What would we do? Where on earth might we live freely? Teaching is my vocation. I have no other means of supporting myself. You are a married woman. Don't you see what would happen if we—'

'Became lovers?' she interrupted.

I felt myself blush. 'Exactly. It would ruin our lives. The lives we live here, anyway.'

'I don't care,' she insisted.

'Well, I do. We both have too much of value to throw everything away.' I could see her face grow hot with frustration. 'Lysette, have you ever had a . . . a passionate friendship with another woman?' I asked gently.

She shook her head. 'No. Never. But I have longed for it always, as long as I can remember.'

'Well, you see, we differ in this respect, for I have had this type of relationship.' I grabbed a poker and stoked the fire. As the kettle began to boil, I searched for fresh tea leaves. 'The world does not treat people like this very kindly, you know,'

I warned her. 'It takes tremendous courage to live as an invert, to defy so brazenly the laws of society.'

'Yes, I imagine that must be true,' she said slowly.

How I wished I could tell her everything, but I didn't dare. What if she told someone else? There were professors, men mostly, and the Board of Governors, people who I'm certain suspected both my suffragette leanings and my sexual identity. There were people who did not want to see a woman succeed, even in the relatively unimportant field of teaching useless things to other women.

'Lysette, let me explain the accepted view on this condition. There are men and there are women,' I said as I handed her the cup of tea. 'They come together, cleave unto each other, and create children. Now, occasionally something occurs which is called an inversion, in which men mistakenly cleave unto other men. This "accidental cleaving" was invented by the ancient Greeks, scholars I believe. In fact they even wrote poetry about it. The Greeks I mean, not the scholars.' I paused, letting the information sink in. I took a long smooth drink of tea, hoping to steady my nerves. 'Inverted relationships have been illegal in Britain since the time of Henry VIII. Oscar Wilde was crucified under such an act. In fact, the penalty for such a crime was death, up until 1885. Now it's merely life in prison.'

'Horrible, horrible,' Lysette mused, shaking her head.

'Most horrible,' I concurred.

'Well then,' she said, seeming calmer and continuing to eat biscuits, 'what causes this inversion?'

I relished the chance to continue our conversation along more scientific lines. 'There are two theories; the acquired, which says inversion is the result of some illness or traumatic experience; and the innate, which believes inversion is inborn. The acquired theorists consider inverts criminals who should be locked up in jail, while the innate theorists believe inverts are lunatics, who would be better served by being studied in a hospital or asylum. In fact,' I said, going to my bookshelf and taking down a mahogany-covered medical volume, 'a well-respected Russian sexologist believes this disease to be, quote "the result of damage to the parents' genes, due to alcoholism, anaemia, debauchery, climate, or high altitude."' I put that book back on the shelf and pulled down the well-thumbed leather volume I consulted so often. 'Dr Karl Westphal says that inversion is due to, quote, "moral insanity resulting from congenital reversal of sexual feelings, marked by cerebral anomalies and functional signs of degeneration."'

I re-emphasised the word 'degeneration', then looked up at Lysette. 'So you must appreciate the gravity of this position,' I told her.

She shook her head as a few biscuit crumbs tumbled into her lap. 'But those are only men you're talking about,' she said warily. 'You've said nothing about inverted women.'

'Yes. You are correct, of course.' I turned to her again. 'Women inverts don't theoretically exist. Queen Victoria said so herself.'

'Well, perhaps she just never met the right one,' Lysette offered, smiling slyly.

I tried to guide her off that path of thought. 'Think of it this way, Lysette. Men have, as a necessary addition to their bodies, sexual appendages which they use to have sexual "acts". Women have no appendages, and are therefore incapable of sexual acts. Unless of course we are having them with men, and then only with our husbands. Unless of course, we are prostitutes. Which we are not. So, scientifically, we can not be inverts.'

Lysette nodded again, pausing to consider the information.

'That sounds logical enough, I will grant you that. But it still doesn't explain my feelings—'

I interrupted her. 'Lysette, in 1901 Richard von Krafft-Ebing, a famous sexological scientist, determined there were only fifty confirmed cases of inverted females, or "lesbians", anywhere in the world. It is unlikely that you would be one of those fifty.'

She shook her head and her long golden curls brushed against her shoulder. 'I don't care what scientists say. I get these dreams sometimes, in which I kiss and touch and . . .'

'Lysette, you cannot afford to give in to those sensations,' I said sternly. 'I know only too well what may result. What of your husband? Have you forgotten your wedding vows, and your wifely duty to him?'

She shook her head with resignation. The tea in her cup jumped and trembled, nearly spilling on to her skirt. 'No. I remember my wifely duty. And my duty to the nation and the Empire to produce strong sons. I know my duty. But it is not love. I do not love him.' She looked down as a tear slid from her eye. 'Tranby, I cannot find it in my heart to love my husband. When I think of Malcolm, I am filled with nothing but cold and hollow indifference. When he is close to me, my heart beats quickly, not for love, but for fear and dread and horror. I cannot bear it. I cringe to sleep beside him every night. I would rather die than be his wife a moment longer.' She sighed, and her nineteen-year-old face took on the hardened features of a much older woman. 'I try to be a good wife, to be the "angel in the house", as you've instructed us. I've been told that is my calling. I learned it as a child in the Snowdrop Band, in the Purity League meetings, in the stories I read in *Girl's Realm* . . .' Her voice trailed away. 'But this life is unbearable. What can I do?'

Run away with me, Lysette. We could stow away on a voyage to the North Pole, and no one would recognise us beneath our leather *work clothes, our ice picks, and our thick winter skins* . . . I heard this strange siren song echoing in my head, but the words on my tongue sounded so very different. 'Go home and be your husband's wife. Share his bed and bear his children,' I said simply.

'Is that your only advice?' she asked, not bothering to wipe away the tears that clung to her chin and jaw, quivering indecisively as if unwilling to part from her lovely face. How I longed to comfort Lysette, to grab each tear and smash it in my hand, then kiss the pain out of her swollen features.

'Yes. I'm afraid so. It is the prudent thing to do.'

'But it feels so desolate,' she said as her voice broke and her stiff collar quivered with the violence of her tears.

'I know it is. But your feelings will ease over time, trust me.'

She drew in a deep breath and composed herself, straightening her jaw and pulling up the edges of her gloves. 'So how can I change the way I feel? I see these images sometimes, of women dancing undressed near a fountain, eating grapes and brushing one another's hair,' she said. I must have looked shocked. My head shot up and she blushed nervously, furiously stirring her tea. My surprise was not at her words, only at how similar her vision was to a long-held fantasy of my own, a beautiful vision of long-legged women moving like nymphs; gleaming, sleek-haired, dancing in an evening mist.

'Well, Lysette, perhaps we need to get to the root of your feelings,' I offered. 'Scientists believe that women have thoughts of a sexual nature only when some kind of energy is out of balance within their bodies. Have you played any lawn games recently? Maybe a bracing round of battledore and shuttlecock?' I asked.

'Games? No,' she said.

'Gentle callisthenics?'

'No. Nothing of the sort.'

'Lysette, have you engaged in any activity sufficiently taxing enough to leave you winded?'

She blushed. 'I do like to run sometimes,' she whispered slowly, looking up at me through the pale fringe of her eyelashes.

'Run?' I asked in disbelief. 'Run?' I did not know adult women were capable of running. I certainly had not run since I passed my menarche many years ago. The thought alone was too exciting, all that rearrangement of the limbs, all that motion in the chest and upper body.

'I like to run, in our garden mostly. I loved to run when I was a little girl, and I imagine I never outgrew it. I take off my shoes, fold down my stockings, loosen my corset and just run, through the grass, with my arms stretched wide. Oh, it feels so good, running wild as the horses on a farm. I run so fast that my feet barely touch the ground, and my skin feels wet and fresh . . .'

I had to stop her before the tingling in my body threatened my very life. I had to stop her speaking; I had to make her leave before my will broke and I decided to follow her everywhere. 'I think we've found the problem. You must give up running. Too much exercise is a leading cause of boyish exuberance in young women.' I grabbed a piece of paper off my desk and scribbled 'Do not run!' as if it were an apothecary's prescription, then pushed the paper into her hands. 'Do not run, not even to catch a train. Take no exercise whatsoever. You must rest more, and quiet your body at once,' I instructed carefully. 'I'm sorry, but I have another appointment, so I'm afraid I must ask you to leave.'

She considered me for a moment, then slowly nodded her head. 'Very well then,' she said. 'I'm sorry for your sake, but

I think I understand you.' She stood and straightened herself, drying the final tears with the edges of the handkerchief. 'Thank you for your help. I will try not to run.' She took my hand in a firm handshake and I felt the heat of her skin, even through the gloves. She leaned in as if she might kiss me on the cheek, and my skin burned in preparation of receiving that blessing, but instead she squeezed my fingers and released. 'So I assume,' she said, 'I won't be able to meet with you again.'

'That would probably be for the best,' I replied. 'The best thing for both of us, really.'

'I see. Thank you again,' she said curtly, then turned and left my office. I heard her footsteps quicken as she moved down the corridor, but then she slowed, perhaps heeding the advice not to be overly active.

I went to the window, and as I watched her progress down High Holborn, I felt something crushing my insides, like a boulder rolling over my soul. '*Lysette Lysette Lysette,*' I whispered, '*come back and let me explain. I did not want to hurt you. Please come back.*' I watched as her image, her broad hat and folded bustle, grew smaller and smaller, before being swallowed in the mouth of the hungry crowd. *Lysette. Please.* The words against the glass beat as soft as moth's wings, like a tender creature desperate to break its cage, and the draught through the crack tickled my ribs.

I was struck by the thought that Lysette might never return to my class, and I feared I would have to feed my soul on memories of our few encounters. My aching dream-visions had reached their completion, and now I could allow my imagination time to rest. I tried to cheer myself with the thought that in England things happen for the best, and manners and good breeding had no doubt averted many a romantic and Italianate tragedy.

'Successful meeting?' Miss Fickle asked pointedly as I left the Institute that evening.

'Very productive,' I replied quietly, centring the strap of my heavy work bag over my shoulder and letting my black scarf drape heavily around my eyes.

'If you ask me, she seems to need quite a bit of personal attention, that one does,' Miss Fickle said, rapping her knuckles against the doorway. 'If you ask me.'

My lovely Lysette – Tonight I contact you from Africa; deepest, densest Africa, where even the darkness can't hide the force of my desires, can't obscure my search for the great jewel of courage. I will find you, I will love you, and I will bring you home.

Most of the men have camped down for the night, but a few sturdy souls work on, slicing through the jungle in hopes of carving out a path by sunrise. Flies buzz angrily just outside the compass of my skull, while I crouch under a veil of sticky mosquito netting and listen to the noises in the distance, the drums and the pounding bass voices that sing so starkly and so wild. A campfire smoulders in the centre of our circle of tents, and a sickly sweet scent rises from the flames; a scent, soaked into the wood, which kills the insects but makes the men homesick. The flames sometimes smell like vanilla, and other times like stewing berries about to be jam; a smell overwhelming with all the ripe dolour of a long English summer. Someone sings a gentle Welsh hymn and even the trees bend forward, seeming ready to weep.

I lie still and fill my head with thoughts of you, even as I listen to the hiss of poison-tipped arrows flying over my tent. Rats and fire ants race across my face, tickling my eyelids and skirting the curved edges of my ears.

A river glistens close by the camp. I glance out over the rippled surface and catch sight of the bloated bodies of smallpox victims, who have been hastily flung into the stream. Their faces gape like witnesses to some obscene horror as they silently bob by. Even in this relentless heat I shiver, shiver out of fear, and out of desire, for I long to have you here beside me, pressing against my arm and breathing the same fetid air. The jungle is so black, so heavy, so full of moisture and passion and need. This excites me, but I am frightened. This is not what I expected when I imagined my own Africa, when I lovingly played with names like Zambezi, like Congo, like Ujiji, and Bulayo, and Maputu Gorge; when I let those strange names twist and turn my lips into the shape of the most exquisite kisses.

Lysette, I think about the two of us drifting down the Nile, stopping to watch the sun settle for a moment like a burnished ball, then dip with a sizzle out of sight as the blue dusk wafts and fans across the water. Plumes of evening smoulder, staining and burning our eyes, and that would be the sign that night had fallen, and we could turn away from the world and look inward, directing our thoughts towards the task of pleasuring each other.

A strange bird calls in the distance. His note of longing floats overhead briefly then descends into a reverie, before losing itself deep in the trees. I can still hear the drumming in the distance, but it waxes and wanes now like a late summer moon, sometimes seeming closer, other times, much further away. The breeze shifts and the scent of clay and rain rises up around my legs as the sweet fire flickers and suddenly burns out.

The men scramble to revive the flames, anxious not to be alone under the black canopy of night. But I love the darkness, and the freedom it brings me, here where I live without fear. I stretch out my hand and imagine you beside me, while I pretend not to smell the rotting little river, upon whose banks dead men pile up, snagging their limbs in nests of swollen weeds and silken rushes. I laugh at myself in the dark, and the frame of my chuckle sticks in the fabric of the blanket. I feel a strong urge to creep out of my tent and explore a while longer, but I dare not move, not while a strange creature with green eyes breathes near my feet and watches me, patient for my first mistake. I dare not move, but must be satisfied with knowing that what I search for might be very close to me now, it might be flowing just beyond the edges of my tent, and I might be missing it; just as I might be missing you, by only inches in the dark.

April ended, May began, and life continued at my quiet flat in Camberwell, with only my feverish midnight writings to keep me company. My cats, Happiness and Bliss, ignored me as always, and I was careful to carry my chin tucked in and my eyes cast downwards. I pressed the books in my arms close to my breasts, so the eye of my heart might be blunted, unable to look out at the harsh and hopeless world. I went on Mercy Missions to the dark alleys of the East End, delivering used books and thin soup and temperance pamphlets. I volunteered my time at the Esperance Club and at the St Pancras Workhouse for elderly women. Our Society was reduced to five spinsters and three gentlewomen-in-need, after we lost one spinster to a hasty marriage, and two gentlewomen to death.

I still attended my suffrage meetings, where the tone had changed dramatically; some of my colleagues were demanding we resort to violence. Several members suggested we borrow the methods of the Salvation Army, tossing away all lady-like behaviour and taking to the highways to change the nation's mind. Someone in the back of the hall whispered that eighty per cent of all men were known to be infected with gonorrhoea, and that led to a small fringe taking up the chant of 'Freedom For Women, Celibacy For Men'. I took notes without responding to the arguments on either side; I could think of nothing but Lysette, and the violence of thrown bricks and letter-bombs meant nothing compared to the emptiness of a life without her.

Lysette did in fact continue to attend my class, which caused me to suffer a kind of tormented joy. It was almost unbearable to see her every Tuesday, to stand before her for an hour but never to be able to speak to her, never be close enough to smell her perfume or to see my breath disturb her hair. I was close enough to see her face, but never near enough to watch the black pupil blossoming in the centre of her eye.

I thought about Lysette without respite, and my longing for her grew deeper and more intense as the days went by. The end of spring brought a re-birth of desire, desire which had lain dormant for many years. Seeds which were long frozen crept silently through the soil and broke into the light. I had been satisfied for so long. Not happy, but satisfied. Life had been infinitely livable, and the world seemed to me a pleasant place. But now I was tempted to look back at my past with different eyes and condemn that old, smug, satis-fied self as empty, shallow, even cruel. I wanted to love Lysette, to dive headlong into love with her and let the rest of the world dry up and disappear. But my heart simply would not allow it, and that passion was a door which had to remain unopened.

Agnes was still ill, but she rallied, and regaled me twice a week with stories of her younger days, of the times when she was pelted with sour fruit, rotten eggs, and shocking obscenities for daring to speak out publicly in favour of rights for women. Her body grew weaker, but almost as a kind of compensation, her mind took flight. She found joy in the smallest objects and gained the ability to remember everything, even as I lifted her in my arms and moved her from bed to chair to bed, bathed her with a sponge, and brushed her tufts of dandelion hair. We developed the strange intimacy of care-giver and care-receiver. The more personal my attention to her, the more formal our conversation. Only when she was clean and dry and wrapped up by the fire did she spin her fabulous tales. How I envied her past; not her future, of which she could only have very little. Yet her spirit was so large and galloped so madly, at times she seemed able to encompass the world. She talked often of Lady Janet Somerville, an aristocrat's daughter and friend of her youth, with whom she spent many lovely summers in Siena, living off an income from the small sketches they sold to tourists.

'The sun, Tranby, the sun,' Agnes would insist, lifting her arm to her forehead, 'turned us as brown as savages and blistered our lips. The hot stones split the soles of our naked feet, and oh, how we laughed when we returned home, and our fathers said we had abused our good looks and would never find husbands.'

It was five o'clock in the evening on 14 May and I was giving up work for the week, packing away my bottles of ink and my last few packets of lecture notes, and turning my thoughts towards an evening spent reading about the Patagonian giants who danced like madmen and covered themselves with dust. My insides ached as always, but this time I knew for certain the source was hunger. I had been fasting once a week and sending the money I saved to the WSPU to help support the suffragists languishing in prison. The rain slipped and plopped outside my broken window, and I dreamed of escaping the confines of my life, of dressing like a boy and stowing away on some enormous cargo ship bound for exotic ports of call. I wanted to be like Baré, who disguised herself as a valet and journeyed with de Bougainville on his global circumnavigation in 1766. When Baré was ultimately revealed to be a woman, de Bougainville was more amused with her than angry, saying, 'She knew when we embarked that we were going around the world, and that such a voyage had raised her curiosity.' I envied Baré and her unwritten story, the secret adventures of the first woman to have done something as extraordinary as circling the world.

Suddenly I looked up and Lysette was standing in the doorway. I blinked several times, afraid to believe she was real. Here before me was Lysette McDonald, not as a dream vision but as a living human being, in a hat with ostrich feathers, a pleated dress, and a stiff collar with a serious frill. She carried on her face the certainty of expression one would only expect on the face of a much older woman. Our eyes met but we said nothing. She stepped into the office and with the tip of her umbrella tapped the door closed behind her without turning around. She took another step closer to me, never breaking eye contact. I stood stock still, while every nerve in my body jumped upright and danced on end. The noise of the rain through the crack in the window grew louder and more menacing.

'We mustn't do this,' I said, as my body trembled.

'I know,' she said, moving closer.

'It's horrible . . .'

'Most horrible,' she replied. Then she smiled. 'The horror kept me awake last night. All night, thinking and tossing and turning . . .'

'My poor child. You poor thing,' I said soothingly. 'How may I help?'

She removed her hat and unpinned her hair so it fell freely, unrolling past her shoulders. 'I'm so cold and so wet,' she said, not smiling, fingering her damp collar and offering me a clear invitation.

'We shall have to see to that,' I said briskly, as I crossed the few steps between us. I put my hands on her shoulders and as she leaned near to me, our faces collided. I drew back and laughed, then I kissed her cheek, and as she turned, her mouth found mine. The first sensation was painful; a searing, biting guilt, but then I felt the melting ache of pleasure. Suddenly I was Leif Ericsson in Greenland, lifting the dew off the grass, holding it to my mouth and realising that nothing on earth had ever tasted quite so sweet. I had no map to guide me forward, but my body found what it searched for, and we kissed and kissed until a wet rose bloomed on my shrivelled old lips, and a sound, both hungry and satisfied, rose from my throat.

'You're still cold,' I said to Lysette, feeling her skin shiver beneath my hands. I slid off her coat and half-jacket and found she was soaked straight through her silken camisole. 'Let me see to this straight away as well.' I opened my black shawl and dress and undid my shirt front while she loosened her corset, and I pulled her closer to me, until the heat of my body lifted into hers, and we stood, chest to chest.

'Oh Tranby, I have wanted so badly to feel your arms around me,' she whispered.

'Yes, Lysette, yes. But not nearly so much as I have wanted you,' I said, fingering her earlobe. I felt the beat of her heart echoed by my own, and I was determined never to let her go as the sting of each kiss settled in my skin.

'Why didn't you kiss me that first day in your office?' she

whispered, letting the reproach sting my ear. 'Didn't you know how much I wanted you to?' She pulled back a few inches and her flushed face steadied into focus. I pulled her close to me again.

'Oh Lysette, how could I? You are my student, and I never expected you to be this thing, to be what I am,' I said, nearly in tears as I stopped her mouth with my own, drinking in the heat from her throat. *Just let it be magic, just let it be magic, let me have one more chance.* The words in my head ran like a chant, and I longed to apologise for all the lying, the denying, and the loneliness; to confess, to fast and ask for forgiveness, to kneel at the altar of this fine and brilliant being, to be willing to forego all other gods for her.

'Didn't you guess that I longed to have you?' she asked desperately, and I shook my head no, then yes, then no again, feeling uncertain, knowing only that I wanted to make this instant last for ever; I wanted to be bare and naked and trembling. I longed to be completely reborn, and dancing endlessly before the vision of this mystical Lysette.

That evening as I returned home, I was certain my acts were written on my skin, and the eyes of every stranger felt bright, ready to indict me for my sin. 'I have done it now,' I told myself, 'I have given in to my most dangerous desires. My colleagues will revile me. If they find out, they will deem me unfit to teach.' But there was comfort enough in the hum of Lysette's kisses that still vibrated on my lips and quivered with the rhythm of my heart. When I reached my flat I was too excited to sleep, so I filled myself with gulps of sweet madeira and doses of calomel. I was too afraid to think about what I had done, too thrilled to pray, and too frightened to weep, so instead I sat at my desk and stared into the candle, whose flame was stronger than I'd ever seen it, firm and fiery and cinnamon-scented, as it filled me with giddy, tickling light. I dipped my nib in ink, and wrote this note, which consisted of the first honest words I had dared to write in years:

> *Lysette*, at last the yoke is lifted, and I can spill free, at least on this page, my soul's true essence. So you do reciprocate, which is more than I dared hope for. My feelings are not aimless arrows as I feared, missing their invisible mark by miles. I have found you now, my lovely one, and I have no intention of letting you go until I have caught you in my arms one hundred times, and tasted the best and most intense of your kisses.

PART THREE

'Say that upon the altar of her beauty you sacrifice your tears, your sighs, your heart.'

The Two Gentlemen of Verona

CHAPTER SIX

After the joy of our first real kiss, which had been racy but chaste, a flurry of doubts descended on me, like a nest of nibbling pigeons pecking through Trafalgar Square. Lysette and I met twice weekly, and after each encounter I told myself I could not allow our relationship to continue. Desire bubbled inside me, as unsettled and uncertain as a phosphate. I was risking my professional reputation. What could I do? I consulted my astrolabe, my sextant, my compass and my chronometer, those trustworthy instruments that did not fly on the tides of emotion, but they told me nothing, and I was left to explore this unknown world all alone. Could this be love? Did I love Lysette? And if I did truly love her, why was I still so frightened?

And anyway, Lysette could not love me. Certainly not me. I, Miss Tranby Quirke, was plain, shapeless, and invisible. The looking-glass tormented me, throwing back at me the image of a sour face with a withered and prickly old mouth. I forced myself to look at my naked body for the first time in four years, and that last time I can assure you had been for purely medical purposes, and I saw the same knobby, unfeminine form that had greeted my eyes years earlier. My stiff hands were still too prim, and had the unpleasant pallor of bloodlessness. My hair, which I trimmed myself with tailor's scissors, was dull and flat, and brown, an insubstantial colour. She did not love me. Lysette could not love me. I felt the words like a hammer tapping into my bones and soul: *She could not love me. Tran-be. Fool. She could not love you.*

And I tried to tell myself that I did not love her; not more than would be prudent anyway, not more than reason, certainly not more than would be proper between a friend and her friend.

I hid my predicament from the world, living my day-to-day life in much the manner I always had. I continued to see to the personal needs of Agnes, who grew weaker and wilder, at times nearly blind with pain, and railing endlessly against present, but invisible, ills. She often called out to Lady Janet, bidding her to take her arm, to keep her head above the water. 'Janet, Janet, don't leave me here, don't leave me here to die.'

'Everything is fine, Agnes,' I would reply, patting her hand and straightening the lace cap, which each week had fewer wiry grey hairs beneath it.

My suffrage work continued too. Although too terrified of crowds to join the march on Parliament, I helped create hundreds of calico banners, painting 'Votes for Women' in shoeblack with a certain panache. I still slept in my creaky bed curled up with my beloved explorers – Burke and Wills, and Livingstone, and El Draco himself, Sir Francis Drake, the men who spoke to me from between the calfskin-bound covers of books whose corners jabbed into my skin while I slept. My midnight automatic writings were filled with images of Cipangu, Eldorado, and the Spice Islands, but always I awoke with the certainty of having dreamt of Lysette. Happiness and Bliss, my

two rogue fellows, woke me belligerently, stirring and stretching and begging for milk, assaulting me with their thinness as
they paraded past me on their way to hunt small birds. My life
was as stable, as pure, and as careful as it had ever been, and yet
I was tormented during these days; nervous, obtuse, suffering
endless intestinal distress. Perhaps some part of me knew the
danger of my actions, and the imminence of my death.

'Has he gone?' I felt the hot whisper of my own breath against
the wooden door. The thin smoky gaslight from the corridor
inched into the darkened flat and found my feet, turned
inward like guilty prisoners.

'Yes.' Lysette's single word slithered in response. Still I did
not open the door, although I felt her presence, the pressure of
her weight against the wood.

'Are you certain?'

'Yes. Tranby, let me in. It's cold out here.'

'When will he be back?' I asked, allowing in only enough
light that Lysette's shadowed features loomed into view.

'The day after tomorrow. Tranby . . .'

'Did anyone see you as you came in?'

She sighed. 'Oh yes. Dozens of people. Why, there was a
parade down Coldharbour Lane! Let's see, I saw Mr
Westonbury, Miss Fickle, all of the Hambleton family, and the
majority of the Board of Governors. They asked me where I
was headed, and I said, "Why, I'm on my way to a secret
rendezvous with Miss Tranby Quirke, of course."' She
paused. 'May I come in now?'

'Sorry. I just had to be certain, you understand. If anyone
finds out about this . . .' I tried to explain, but she embraced
me and stopped my mouth with a kiss, and my fear lifted
briefly as I dissolved in her arms.

'Would you care for some coffee?' I asked, breaking the

embrace. I moved towards the fireplace and my table display of small trinkets; the burlap sack of coffee beans, the china saucers, my mermaid-shaped teaspoons from Copenhagen. All week I had been practising how to tell Lysette no, how to resist her with dignity, to hold back from rushing into lust.

'No coffee. We can have that later.' She pulled me back into her arms. 'Tranby, hurry, hurry please. Let's get on with it. I've been waiting all week to see you, I can't bear to wait a moment longer.' She rubbed my shoulders and pulled at my shawl. Her eyes were anxious, her fingers busy, and her lips pulsing pink. Hers was a youthful hunger, not embittered by disappointment. She made me realise that I had never been young.

'Here?' I asked.

'Yes. Here.'

'Very well then,' I said, unable, or at least for the moment unwilling, to argue. We undressed quickly and without cere-mony, leaving our layers of clothing scattered in stiff heaps near our feet. I was ashamed, true, but not too ashamed. My only concession to good taste was to turn the photograph of my father towards the wall. As I stood before Lysette unclothed, I was embarrassed by my thinness and unfemininity, and the brown shadows lining my ribs.

'Is this what you were waiting for?' I asked sarcastically, touching my breasts. 'Is this it?'

'It is. And this. And this,' she said confidently, taking me in her arms, and I began to feel better. This was what it felt like to find unchartered islands. This was the bliss of Columbus, of possessing the first steps on solid land after months of only salt air and salt water.

We kissed and pressed closer, and Lysette folded her arms around me, as if to protect my skin from the unkind air, and I warmed beneath her gentle weight.

'More, give me more,' I asked suddenly, surprised by my outburst as I begged for her to give me not only her arms but everything, kisses and lips and tongue tips, and I was afraid I was frightening her, so honest was my need, so powerful the cry that was collecting inside me, massing force like storm clouds beneath my skin.

Lysette responded as her lips, proud and thick and higher-set than my own, brushed the narrow bridge of my pinched little nose. My hands followed her outline from the bell-shaped bird cage of her ribs, secreting her songbird heart, down to the tipped slopes of her hips. Her breasts pressed against my collar bone, so I submitted to her, yielding as new juices suddenly flowed through me, tasting as sharp as tin and minerals, and I knew what Pytheas was looking for when he found his 'Ultima Thule', the peak, the northernmost point.

'Yes, Lysette, yes,' I whispered, as I searched her body for an open place, a Straits of Magellan broad enough to let me pass through. I wanted to find that warm and unknown ocean, Pacifica, which I knew to be hiding just out of sight, as I slid down her body, down the dented path that ran, firm as a peach, from the notch of her sternum, between her breasts and her ribs to her tender stomach. Her soft cries guided me forward as she steadied my shoulders. I went deeper and deeper, finding the hidden recesses waiting to be filled. She buffeted me like a loose ship tossed against the rocks, pushing faster and faster until I felt as if the slightest flick might split her open, might divide her up the middle like a great tree split and sparking, smouldering after being hit by lightning. Suddenly she crested, then dissolved into my arms.

'I love you, I love you, I love you, Tranby Quirke,' she said between long draughts of breath.

I quivered as I held her close to my naked chest. 'I know, I know, I know,' I answered. I waited until my heart had slowed enough that my reply of, 'I love you too, Lysette,' was the only sound I heard. '*Primus circum,*' I added, and felt the echo in the rattling windows of the baker's shop beneath us. '*Primus circumdedisti me.*'

'What?' she asked, finding her voice.

'*Primus circumdedisti me,*' I whispered. 'What the earth said to Ferdinand Magellan. You are the first to have circumnavigated me.'

Afterwards we sat quietly in my library, and she shone like a bright jewel among my many little things; my father's books and wine decanters, the plump cushions, the Italian cut glass and the recently acquired Victrola. We whispered and laughed, and I smiled at the sight of her dove-white skin. We drank the spiced Malaysian coffees and lighted my most precious candles from the lands of Araby.

'Tell me a story. An adventure story,' Lysette asked, leaning back and letting her eyelids grow heavy.

'All right then,' I said, opening my mind to the catalogue of travels that lay inside, coiled and patient, like cobras ready to rise and strike. 'The year is 1512, and I am a captain in the army of Balboa. We march our men and our bloodhounds into the jungles of Panama, which are full of mynah birds, tree frogs, and screaming howler monkeys. At Balboa's side rides the wardog Leoncico with his many battle scars, the dog who wears a solid gold collar and collects a soldier's pay. After marching for seven weeks, we reach Comogran village, where the leader offers us a feast of smoked venison, and maize beer in gold-trimmed gourds, and he gives us each two native girls who bathe five times a day and rub their naked bodies with perfumed ointments.'

'That sounds lovely,' Lysette purred, patting her stomach with satisfaction.

'Oh, but it isn't,' I said suddenly, surprising myself as a bolt of fear lit my mind. 'It isn't lovely at all. You see, Lysette, when we cross the Isthmus of Panama, we find a hidden village whose chief keeps a harem of handsome young men dressed in women's garments. That butcher Balboa, horrified by what he considers this evidence of mortal sin, sets loose Leoncico and the other dogs, and no one can stop him; he does not call back his dogs until every boy is slaughtered, torn to pieces, torn to shreds. As I stride across that bloody battlefield where no battle has taken place, I weep bitter tears too weak to dilute the pools of blood, and I know then that inverted love exists everywhere, and is everywhere feared; in every place it lives it sits vulnerable, ripe for destruction. Here it is killed before I can protect it, struck down like those rows of tender, green-twig boys.'

Lysette looked at me and her eyes filled with tears. 'All of them? All murdered?' she asked.

'Yes. Every last one.' I saw in my mind's eye the mist of their last breaths, rising and settling like dew upon the grass.

'No, I don't believe it,' Lysette insisted. 'Surely one survived. Or two. Yes, two, who loved each other so very much. I'm certain they ran away, into the forest, deep into the trees, and they live there still.' She smiled bravely. 'Just like you and I. We will escape. We will break free one day. Tell me something else,' she asked suddenly. 'Tell me what it is like to go to France, to those special clubs where tall women meet to smoke cigarettes and speak of driving motorcars.' Her green eyes glistened as she burrowed her shoulders deeply into the soft cushions and her hair feathered gently around her face.

'If only I could, Lysette. But I have never been to France.'

'But surely, you've been there . . .' she said, sitting forward.

'A thousands times, at least. But only in my midnight writings.' I took the chair across from her and told the sorry story. 'I nearly went to Paris. Once. I had my ticket. I took the train to Dover, and then a taxi motor car to the docks, and there I saw my ferry, standing tall and white and proud. *La Merielle*, that was her name. I remember thinking what a lovely name that was for a ship. *La Merielle* – my freedom, my escape, my adventure. I stood on the dock waiting to board, with my carpetbag under my arm. It was a bit windy, and the ship rocked and rocked and I tried to ignore it, but my eyes and my stomach couldn't keep up with all that rocking. My head began to twirl and I felt faint as I watched the long queue of women boarding the ship. They dipped and swayed on the wooden stair, and their arms swung side to side as they struggled to hold on to their hats, and if their hats blew off it seemed certain they themselves would be blown into that green rocking sea, and their skulls would be dashed to pieces against those high white cliffs, and suddenly I could not continue. I couldn't get aboard that ship. That is the sad truth, Lysette. I was incapable of boarding a little ferry full of happy grandmothers for a twenty-three-mile journey. I am no explorer. I am nothing but a cowardly failure. I knew then that the only journeys I would make would be the ones inside my mind.'

Lysette stood quickly and moved to my side, in her haste nearly tipping the small ashwood table. She cupped my head in the largeness of her hands and tilted my face towards hers. 'Oh Tranby, I'm so sorry. Come here and let me comfort you. You mustn't feel so bad about it.' She led me to the sofa and dutifully I sat down. She stroked my cheek and held me close, reassuring me with her gentle voice.

'You *are* an adventurer, at heart. You'd sail to the South Pole if it were possible.' She paused. 'You'd do it for me, I know you would.' I was surprised she didn't pity me for my need of conceit. In her eyes, I think revealing my weakness made me somehow more human, more worthy of concern. 'You were just afraid,' she said. 'There's no shame in being frightened.'

'But are you not angry that I lied to you?' I asked. 'I let you believe that I had travelled to so many places.'

'No. I'm not cross. In fact, I think I love you more than ever.'

'But now you see how weak I am,' I insisted.

'Perhaps, but you've let me into your heart. Tranby, when I first came to your class, I was taken by your strength, your intelligence. I was amazed by the way you carried yourself, the way you walked into the classroom with your head held high, as if you weren't ashamed to be a woman, you weren't ashamed to speak to everyone about the ideas in your head. But now I can love you for your weaknesses too. I can love you for showing me more of yourself,' she said.

'I fear that doesn't count for very much,' I told her.

'Tranby, that counts for more than anything else.'

I was so close to her that I could feel the warmth of my breath against her skin, and the faint pulsing in the palms of her hands. 'You see, Lysette, I sometimes think I was born to be fearful. I was a weak and sickly only child. My mother died when I was four, and my father died four years ago. My father doted on me, in fact he used to quote old Capulet, saying, "Earth hath swallowed all my hopes but she." Once I had a terrible fever and was eight months confined to my bed. It would not be melodramatic to say there was some question as to whether I would live or die. I survived, but I was no child afterwards, for by the time I was well, I had learned to read and study and figure numbers and sums, and I had learned to worry, learned that from my father at my bedside, whose great grey eyes constantly foresaw my loss. Lysette, how can I explain the way I feel? It is as if I can not break free from myself, and yet I have this deep need inside me, to travel, to sail far way, to somehow leave this life behind. I have always believed that I was born for something different. For something else.'

She smiled and stroked my forehead. 'I understand,' she said, then she brushed her eyelashes against my cheek in a tickling butterfly kiss that fluttered through my blood. I could have stopped speaking at that point, she did not need me to explain more, but some force, perhaps her kindness, compelled me to continue, bidding me to unwind more of the ribbon of my secret, secret self.

'I wonder sometimes, would I be a different woman if I had not been weaned on fear? I learned to live my life through books and stories, because life was a dangerous thing. Life itself was frightening, an unknown element. Stories of adventures became better than the adventures themselves,' I said bitterly.

'But there are always new worlds to conquer,' she insisted. 'Or else be like Alexander.'

'You remember that?' I asked in amazement, pulling away from her hands.

She smiled. 'Of course. I cling to your words. I cling to whatever you give me.'

'I'm sorry now I have not given you more. You deserve better. Better than what I can give,' I said candidly.

'Don't despair, Tranby, all may yet be well. I imagine we'll have adventures of our own someday.' She kissed me gently but with enough pressure that I felt the fullness of her lips against my cheekbone. 'What was your father like?' she asked.

The question surprised me. I never spoke of him to anyone; I had long ago consigned him to a realm of private contemplation, but suddenly Lysette's love unleashed in me a feverish need to grieve for my father, to remember him, to restore him to his rightful place in my life. 'My father was a wonderful man,' I told her proudly. 'He wasn't a keen conversationalist, and there was a vague air of embarrassment about him. I sometimes thought he felt there was something improper about a man raising a daughter alone, but he was a physician, so at least he had the comfort of knowing he moved in respectable circles.' I smiled at the memory of my father's bluster, his gruff good nature, and loving charm.

'Was he a man of letters? He left you all his big books,' she said, nodding towards the bookcase overstuffed with cheap classic novels and heavy educational texts.

'Oh, I suppose he was, in his own way. Father mistrusted poetry, but he was always keen on Shakespeare. He justified this indulgence by reading Shakespeare as history, never as poetry. To him, there was no music in it. It said what it said.' A dozen memories floated up suddenly from nowhere. This was Lysette's gentle magic, at work on me again. 'When I was ill, he had me perform entire scenes in my sickbed. I could recite a stirring St Crispin's Day speech, and my rendition of Enobarbus' description of Cleopatra moved hearers to tears. I can still see Father and his colleagues arranged like plaster saints along my bedside. Each in turn places an ear to my chest, anxiously evaluating every gurgle or wheeze. I felt so inadequate when I couldn't produce something more interesting than a regular heartbeat and the odd popping cough.' I laughed at the memory; a small thing, so trivial and from so long ago, but Lysette shuddered and wrapped her arms around my waist, pressing the curve of her skull and the folds of her ear into the depths of my chest.

'Tranby, you are so dear to me. Please, don't forbid me to say it. Let me love you more. I want to tell the whole world. My dear one. My love. Let us flee London and start a new life somewhere else.'

I stroked the rich amber waves of her hair, and the pressure of her skull warmed my ribs and soothed the cold parts of my soul as she listened, truly listened, to the mysterious sounds inside my body, which for once sang to someone other than themselves. 'Lysette, my darling one. We will do it. Some day. We will fly this life,' I told her, and I felt the good solid weight of my promise as it tumbled from my lips and echoed in my chest before it drifted down to settle in the softness of her hair.

For twelve weeks Lysette McDonald and I were lovers; honest lovers; the fully, wholly, body-and-soul type of lovers. For the first, and what must surely be the last, time in my life, I experienced something beyond my comprehension, an abyss of confusion, but also something similar to what Oscar Wilde called 'that deep, spiritual affection that is as pure as it is perfect'. And they were the most beautiful twelve weeks of my life, although never, not for a single instant, was I completely free from the shadows of doubt and fear. I was certain I had entered my own Burning Zone, that place so feared by the Phoenicians, that cauldron of death where the sea boiled over steaming coral reefs, and flesh-eating monsters lay in wait on jagged rocks.

My darling Lysette – How can I explain the uncertainty that sometimes bubbles up inside me? I am lost at sea, and every day drifting further and further away from you. It is 1577 and I am in the company of Sir Francis Drake. I am a young girl now, but I have stowed aboard his ship disguised as a boy. I have been working as a valet in name only; mostly my job is to satisfy the oldest soldiers' perverted pleasures, and as unpleasant as that task is, nothing broke my soul so much as reaching the high rough coastline of

Tierra del Fuego, where Sir Francis ordered us to kill 3000 penguin because they walked like children and dressed like little men; and I for my small size was given the job to walk among the steaming carcasses and search their tails and fins for salvageable bullets. I still had not forgiven Sir Francis for this savagery when we landed in New Albion three days ago and Sir Francis, playing the role of the fair-skinned god, blessed the natives with his perfumed waters, and strode out among them to the music of violas, while they cowered in terror and slashed their own skin in a show of horror, shock, and ecstasy, and I tore my clothing into strips for bandages and slipped among them silently as I struggled to bind and heal their gaping, bright-red wounds.

It was only by accident on 17 August, in a damp and musty corridor of the Simperton Institute during a ten-minute break that I heard some girls gossiping about Lysette; saying that she was ill, at home in bed, and was not expected to return to class for several weeks.

'Ill?' I asked nervously as I tried to imagine the impact of weeks without seeing Lysette. 'What is this about Mrs McDonald being ill? What have you heard? Why wasn't I informed?' I grabbed two of the girls by their arms while their companions escaped my clutch, scurrying away. 'Why didn't you tell me?' The girls blanched and trembled, too frightened to twist out of my tight grip.

'I . . . I . . . I don't know, Miss Quirke,' one said softly. 'I don't know if she's ill or not. I just heard some other girls talking, that's all.'

'And what about you? What have you heard?' I shouted at the other girl, whose face grew tight and frightened as I turned her arm.

'Nothing. I swear to you, it was only a rumour,' the girl insisted.

'Well, you shouldn't gossip, it's very bad manners,' I scolded the girls. 'I should give you both a good rap across the knuckles.' But instead I let them loose and hurried back to my classroom. Then I proceeded to do something I had never so much as considered before – I released my students a full hour early, and not only that, I sent them home without any assignments. I told them I didn't mind one bit whether they read Chapter Seven on proper cutlery positioning, and as far as I was concerned, it didn't matter if they neglected to present a calling card when visiting members of the landed gentry, or if they ever again mistakenly ate cheese before five in the evening.

I rushed down the staircase and into the glass-panelled lobby of the Institute, just as Miss Fickle was returning from her midday meal. 'The staff have a meeting at three this afternoon,' she said severely, brushing the last dusting of powdered sugar from her firm upper lip with the edge of her handkerchief. 'You will be presenting your report on the propagation of the Gospel in the Belgian Congo, will you not?' she asked.

'Terribly sorry, we'll have to postpone it,' I called over my shoulder, as I pushed through the door and into the road, nearly stepping into the path of an oncoming motorcar. 'I have an engagement that must be immediately seen to!' Miss Fickle must have thought me possessed by some demon as I hurried down High Holborn, without my coat, one glove missing, and with wild papers darting and flying behind me. Of course I was possessed, but no one would have guessed it; that demon was Lysette, and her secret name was love.

I hurried back to my flat, festering with my need to see Lysette. Once at home I quickly determined it would be best to dress like a boy in order to glide more easily through the streets. I had enjoyed dressing as a boy during my adolescence. Originally I did it guiltily as a tribute to Jonnie, but as I began to enjoy it more and more, I did it simply to please myself, although I gave it up in my mid-twenties, when I decided I was too old for such foolishness.

Wasting no time, I slid myself into a disguise of gaiters, boots, and greatcoat, and hastily pushed my hair into a tight tweed cap. I stuffed my sack with chocolates and forget-me-nots, and a glass phial of sweet fragrance to dab behind Lysette's delicate ears. Having not dressed as a boy for many years, I was especially pleased and relieved to discover that advancing spinsterhood had added naught to my limited repertoire of feminine charms. While I dressed I felt an aching inside myself, a straining in my deepest muscles, a longing to envelop Lysette's flesh and make her disappear within the pit of my neediness.

As I left my flat and strode down Coldharbour Lane, dodging horses, bicycles, and boys behind boxes on wheels, I felt a strange and giddy freedom, and an unaccustomed spring in my step, as if I were en route to a new and better world. I did not hide my face or cover the blush in my cheeks. I did not shrink behind a newspaper or a hastily opened magazine, I did not peer uneasily over the edges of a dog-eared, paperback classic; instead, I held my head high, waving to the match girl and nodding at the muffin man plying his puddings and cakes. My lips parted in the shape of Lysette's name, and as I boarded the train I caught as many eyes as I could. 'Mind where you step, young man,' an elderly woman, teetering with boxes, scolded me as she stepped into my path.

I watched from the train window as the squalor of central London, the endless rows of houses, the grey, faceless crowds, the muddy streets and the slate-coloured sky, gave way to suburban sunshine; the cottages graced with flower beds beneath bay windows, and the walled-in gardens thick with poplar and lilac trees. Gradually the packmen, the piemen, and the poignant-faced orange girls disappeared, their places taken by families with children, serious ladies in serious hats, and old gentlemen held upright by strong wooden canes.

I left the train and walked the last half mile. As I drew closer to Lysette's, I grew careful near Kestrel Close, and when no one was watching me, I slipped myself into the hedgerow across the road, from where I could get a clear view of the front of the house. Suddenly I caught a glimpse of Malcolm in the scullery, gulping down a cup of tea and brushing his mouth with the back of his thick hand. He was a big, broad-bellied man, as Lysette described him, but less ferocious than I anticipated. I had imagined him to be all black coat, bowler hat, big shoulders and thick girth, but in fact his cheeks were round and well oiled, and a scattering of freckles across his broad face gave him an air almost of innocence. His sandy-grey hair was still ginger at the temples and it lay like two flaming streaks aside his head, parted straight, severely back-combed, and liberally greased with macassar oil. The ginger tone continued in his bushy sideburns and droopy mustache, and in his generous eyebrows which rested contentedly over his world-weary eyes. He was not a handsome man, but he was not an ogre either, rather he was a man with a look of well-fed satisfaction and successful business transactions.

I began to hate him. First I hated him simply for being a man, and for having all the opportunities attendant on that fact. Then I hated him for possessing what I desired most, and I hated him for mistreating my rare and precious jewel. Hate is a sickness; it starts so small but soon it infects everything. As I waited in the hedgerow, struggling to stay patient, I felt the hate rise up like a sickly liquid in my throat. Why didn't I kill him? Malcolm would know our secret sooner or later. He would taste me on her mouth, or see me reflected in her eyes. One night she might, I almost hoped, call out my name in her sleep. With his temper, what might happen if he knew the truth? As I shuddered with fear, the hard seed of resolve ripened and fell in my chest. We had to leave. I had to find some means of escape.

A few minutes passed, and I watched as Malcolm, with his small hat and tightly wound umbrella, emerged from the house. He stopped on the step and as he turned back, I saw Lysette behind him in the doorway. She looked pale and tired in a plain, loose-fitting dress, and with her hair brushed but not styled, scattered in loose curls across her shoulders. He leaned in for a kiss but she pushed him away with the heel of her hand. A broad brush-stroke of Scots anger swept to his face. He grabbed her chin and pulled her tight to him, centring her face and crushing her cruelly with a kiss. She stumbled backwards, looking dazed, but then her face sprang to life as she wiped her mouth with a defiant brush of her hand. I grabbed some twigs and broke them in my fingers, pressing down on the anger that told me to lunge from the hedge and kill him on the spot. He strode away adjusting his hat, as Lysette, still wounded, slammed the door closed.

When he was safely out of sight down the road, I let myself in through the garden gate. I hurried to the front door and tapped out an urgent plea for Lysette to let me inside.

She opened the door slowly, peering around the corner as if afraid to find Malcolm. 'Tranby!' she burst out in delight when she realised it was me, and never had my name sounded so lovely.

'Let's go in,' I said quickly, anxious to avoid the neighbours' busy ears and eyes. Just inside the hall we fell into each other's arms, and the weight of her body was beautiful. The feel of flesh on flesh and bone on bone made me realise how empty my arms had been without her. 'When will he be back?' I asked quickly, anxious to make the most of every second we could spend together.

'He's gone up to London, to the pubs,' she answered edgily. 'He won't be back until late tonight.'

'And your maid? Where is she?'

'Malcolm sent her away weeks ago, when she refused his advances. He hasn't found a more willing girl yet.'

At that, I allowed myself to relax in her arms. 'Lysette, I missed you so much today. One day! And it was as if I might never see you again,' I whispered in her ear as her hair tickled my lips. My hands moved up and down her scalp and neck and back, fluttering with disbelief that she was so substantial and so real.

'I've been ill the past few days. Malcolm won't let me leave the house until I'm better. Or until I'm expecting.'

'I'm so sorry,' I said, helping her to a chair and kneeling down beside her. 'When I was waiting outside I watched Malcolm leave. It was all I could do not to run over here and kill him when I saw him hurt you.'

'Oh Tranby, he's been terrible, simply terrible,' she said, rocking back and forth. 'I hate Malcolm so desperately sometimes,' she panted. Her cheeks grew flushed and her fingertips tugged at her throat. I looked around at the dark and flowery furnishings, the Turkish rug, the Japanese embroidery, the Indian brass trays, and all the expensive bric-à-brac intended to soften the walls of her suburban prison.

'Shhh. I'm here with you now,' I murmured, stroking her hair and trying to soothe her. She was weak, probably anaemic. Her full lips were bruised where Malcolm had kissed her, and the wild look of fear in her eyes scared me. I had to get her away from him. 'Let's go upstairs,' I suggested, and she nodded as I helped her up. We took the stairs slowly, pausing to rest at each step.

Malcolm was killing her spirit. He blamed her for not getting pregnant, believed her body was at fault. By marrying Lysette he had purchased the right to the plot between her legs, and he was determined to stake his claim. He would not let that land rest or heal, he would pummel that patch, assault it, strike it, rake it, dig deeper trenches in it until the land itself was barren, and all the earth had been worked into dirt.

'He's going to do it this time. He's threatened to lock me up in this house and force me to get with child,' she said softly as we entered the bedroom and she fell limply into the nearest chair. 'He can't do that. It's not legal, is it? He's only trying to threaten me.'

I took her hand gently and debated whether I should tell her the truth. 'Legally, he is allowed to do that. English law says a husband can sue his wife for restitution of conjugal rights, and then have her imprisoned if she refuses him intercourse.'

She scoffed, throwing her head back. 'I might have guessed,' she said bitterly.

'Legally, yes, he has that right, but morally, no. This is an outrage, Lysette. He'll kill you. Any doctor would agree, a pregnancy in your condition might threaten your very life. Besides, I won't let him do it,' I told her firmly. 'I will take you away.'

'Really? Do you mean it – we may leave?' she asked, as hope lit up the rims of her tired green eyes.

I touched the blueberry welt above her lip, brushing it with my fingertip. 'Yes. We must go soon. Malcolm is destroying you. I can feel it. He's killing you. You are like the petal of a flower, and each time he touches you, he leaves a dead spot shaped like his fist. To my mind, he's handled you too much already.'

'Tranby . . .' She struggled forward but, just as quickly, dropped back into the chair. I could feel the fatigue coming off her skin like a radiating fever. She was tired, down to her soul.

'My poor child. My lovely girl,' I said, stroking her cheek, twirling the golden tendril end of her curls between my fingers and thumb. 'Let's go to bed. Let's rest for a while,' I said, soothing her gently. She leaned back and her eyelids fluttered. Her lips parted, but she was too weary to speak. Sliding one arm behind her back and the other under her knees, with a great burst of strength I lifted Lysette and carried her to the bed. She was surprisingly light, having lost weight in the previous few weeks. The bones in her spine poked into the palm of my hand and the hinged joint of her knee swung freely. Some substance, a spirit, or a liquid sort of hope, was leaking from her being. I could feel it. She was disappearing from me, right before my eyes. If I didn't save her, she would dissolve, worn down into something thinner than silk.

I placed her on the bed, then shifted the satin pillows and the tartan blankets so they covered her body. My arms hurt from lifting her, but a current of strength moved through me. I had to protect her. But for now we could rest, idling an hour or two, quietly dozing in her lacy canopy bed. The early evening sky outside was settling, streaks of light elbowed out by creeping darkness, thumbed down by a deep violet laden with black. I pulled the heavy velvet curtains closed and I lighted several small beeswax candles and arranged them on the marble console beside the bed.

'My darling Lysette,' I whispered as I watched the flames' reflections play on Lysette's sweet face, throwing amber and peach into her paleness, transfiguring her sleep-shrouded image into something restful but coiled, something quiet, but vibrantly alive. I took off my boots and my waistcoat and pulled out the tails of my work shirt. Then I climbed into the bed beside her. I felt large and dusty all of a sudden, and my skin smelled of trains and tobacco, leather and sweat. Lysette turned towards me without opening her eyes, but she opened her arms far enough for me to slide in. I cradled her to my chest, which twinged and buzzed with the strain of the day's activities.

'Lysette. My beautiful girl,' I told her, stroking her hair, feeling each strand as pure and golden as the strings of a harp, and I felt her smile in the darkness as a purr of satisfaction rose from her throat.

'We will find our freedom,' I whispered. 'Even if only in this room. Let Malcolm smell the powerful perfume of two women together, the union that is destined to leave all men out. Let him taste our exclusive kisses, but only second hand. Reject him in his bed, and let him know by how much he has missed your tenderest parts.'

I cannot say how long Lysette and I lay there, because these were moments that occurred outside of time, in a place beyond my limited means of measuring. We were inside a stillness that is eternal and absolute. I was barely breathing, and the earth and all the universe were reduced and distilled to the rareness of the air passing back and forth between our bodies. I felt the hum in my body, and tasted the sweet kisses with which I dressed Lysette's face. I watched the drama unfolding within her knitted eyelids. She spoke an odd language, addressed and collected lost children, resurrected dead friendships. 'Tranby, Tranby,' she called out earnestly, inviting me to her inner life, and just by touching her hand I could join her in that secret, special, and blissfully distant world.

I drifted in and out of sleep for several hours, exchanging my dream of adventures for the reality of opening my eyes and finding Lysette sleeping at my side. This was a dream too sweet to set free, but it released me instead, sending me back to the world of things; my ordered life of teaching, of meetings, of calico banners. 'Someday, it will be like this every evening,' I promised myself. My thoughts were shaken, and finally dispersed, by the sound of men moving through the streets, hunkering home to their wives, jiggling with money and bloated with gin. I checked my pocket watch, which lay warm and smooth beneath me, pressed deep into the softness of the bed. Eleven o'clock. Malcolm would return soon, and I had to steal back home. It suddenly occurred to me that this would not be a difficult journey to make while dressed as a boy. I might even walk safely through St Giles and Seven Dials, if I shielded my face from the hollow, frightened eyes of the prostitutes, who would not realise they had nothing to fear from me.

'Meet me at Hyde Park, Saturday at midday,' I whispered in Lysette's ear, then kissed her good-bye. I rose and slipped unnoticed into the streets, for once grateful to be tied to my black shadow. For the first time in my life I was happy to be invisible, to be nothing but a silent creature moving through the night.

My darling Lysette – We are lost, shipwrecked in a land of merciless savages, and you are being held captive, some-where on the dark side of the island. I have built a hut for us, on the far end of the beach, in a cypress grove free from the swarms of brilliantine spiders, and bursting with mangoes and bushes of nardoo seeds. I bathe naked in the salty spray each morning, and sleep dreaming of you in my rope bed at night. I will find you, I will have you; I will bring you to safety where we will live free and love.

I am returning to the hut with my evening meal; a handful of berries and a wild turkey slung over my shoulder, a large flaccid creature that bleeds against my back. I am tired and aching and my mind is full with thoughts of you. I am inattentive for a moment, but just long enough for a huge clawed creature, with the wings of a bat and the face of a lion, to pounce down on me and wrestle me to the ground. I struggle helplessly but the creature pins me flat, rears back on its hind legs and takes a swipe at my side. And for a brief whirling moment, the world is stunned, swallowed by silence.

My scream shatters the stillness as the creature grabs the wild turkey and shoots away into the trees. I can hear its footsteps through the lush forest, although it is a muffled, fuzzy sound. My ears are fading. I am dying. My chest feels empty, oddly still. There is no rush of air, no pumping blood, only a dark, swift force pulling me out of myself. My hand over my side covers the wound, but does nothing to stop the steady but slowing flow of blood. I wipe my arm on the opposite sleeve and the dark blood spreads quickly through the fabric, staining it nearly black. I wipe and wipe, until the whole of the sleeve is heavy with blood, and a dark pool spreads across the damp tropical grass. I realise, surprisingly, that in fact I long to die. I am ready to leave this world, ready to put all adventures behind me, and find out at last what lurks on the other side.

'Tranby, Tranby!' I hear your voice as you call out to me from beyond the forest. I try to open my mouth but my lips have gone stone cold. I feel myself begin to rise, spiralling upwards, as my spirit scatters and drifts through the trees. My eyes are open, and I am struck by this last vision of my body, soaking in a puddle of blood. You run through the forest, your feet turn up great clumps of green soil, but you will not reach me in time.

'Good-bye, Lysette.' I try to say the words, but your name is too thick to speak out, too solid now, and the word itself lodges inside me like a plum pit caught in my throat, and I know if I dare cough it out, my dying heart will tremble and fall, dropping as careless as a paper blossom. I press my cold fingers against my cold lips to hold them closed as I move higher and higher and higher. Only my tears still feel warm, lukewarm for now; but cooling, cooling and falling away from me, falling and scattering faster than ash.

I awoke on Saturday morning, 21 August, feeling dull and out of sorts. While I was sleeping, a thin liquid had leaked from my eyes and nose, staining the bedsheet beneath my head. My limbs were stiff and aching, and even a cup of strong coffee and the late summer sunshine pouring through my window could not arouse my slumbering blood. At first I attributed my ill feeling to the mild headcold that had plagued me for days, but as I read my automatic writing from the night before, I understood the reason for my unease. Doubt and fear were still inside me; assuageable in daytime, but overwhelming me by night.

As I dressed and readied myself to see Lysette, the uneasiness still clung to me, throbbing like a quiet nerve. It was only a dream, I told myself. I indulged my imagination and pretended that I was meeting Lysette not for the afternoon, but to run away for ever. How simple it would be to pack up my things: a few books, the photograph of my father, a small sack of coins, and a copy of the article I had published in *The Cumberland Monthly Journal of Ladies' Education*. I thought about how lovely Lysette would look in the late summer sunlight as we struggled to the ferry with her luggage in our arms, calling anxiously to the felt-capped boys behind us who would be wheeling steamer trunks and balancing our loose bouquets of daisies. I imagined the glittering blond reflection of Lysette's hair, the brisk breeze fanning her cheeks, the green grass, the stout flowers, and even the sweet birdsong serving as background to our departure. The fantasy made me feel decidedly better, and I left my flat still in a dream-state, thinking foolishly, Perhaps I will never return to this place again. Perhaps this is what it feels like to lock this door for ever, and let everything beneath this roof rot, decay, and crumble to dust, only to be unsealed years later, without any sign that a Tranby Quirke had ever lived at all.

And so, a few hours later, I found myself striding towards Speaker's Corner with a single violet in my hand; single because a dozen would have called attention both to me and to themselves. My gloves, white for once, were spotless and freshly pressed, and I had purchased a stylish new hat especially for the occasion, a large, dark hat with a thick brim, heavy decorative ribbon, and a cluster at the front made of something which resembled dried fruit. I could barely hold my head up, and the pressure on my neck made my shoulders ache, but the pain didn't bother me as I imagined a glamorous version of myself, a Tranby Quirke dressed in fine hats and ivory lace, gliding across a wooden dance floor, swift-footed and confident in her high-buttoned boots. But then, as I turned the corner, a group of three beautiful girls, wide with boxes, bearing stacks of gifts, and dressed in hats much grander than my own, strode into my path. I stumbled as the girls spun past me, and as I struggled to stay upright, I heard them laugh behind my back. I looked up and caught a glimpse of my reflection in a shop window. At first I did not think she could be me – this foolish old woman wearing a hat designed for someone much younger, and clutching one thin flower, a sad emblem of hope. This grey-faced spinster with a young girl's passion, trying to capture an elusive and undeserved love. Pathetic. Pathetic, the word rang in my head, and I longed to run back to my flat and lock myself inside, safe with my books and maps and diagrams.

As I stood at the corner waiting for Lysette, the dab of perfume on my neck began to burn my skin, and my fingers searched for and found several raised welts. At first I was not worried, but then the sun grew fierce and spiteful, and the flower wilted in my fist, turning brown and staining the unsullied glove, and my neck began to sweat and my whole body felt sticky and wet with an overripe odour, a smell that seemed to indict me for something I might be thinking. The streets felt unusually crowded, and every single person seemed to be staring straight through me, condemning me simply for standing there, or for attempting to love. And then I saw Lysette, her high proud head inches above everyone else's, as she knifed through the pack of people and fell into my arms, kissing my forehead and pulling me away from the street and into the park.

'What a glorious day!' she exclaimed, throwing back her head and indulging in a smile, and suddenly everyone and everything else in the world dissolved, save for her.

'Yes,' I told her. 'It couldn't be lovelier.' I wanted to tell her everything, to convey every thought and emotion that had passed through my head since the night before. I wanted to chart for her the rising and falling rhythm of my faith, how at times I felt I could stop the earth with my love for her, and how, at other times, I was frightened of my own shadow, so frightened of life itself that I had not the courage to reach for her hand. I wanted to say all those things, but my brain was stubborn and my throat remained closed. Lysette was bright and happy, and I couldn't bear to force on her my doubts and my unhappiness. As we strolled through the park, we saw elegant ladies on sleek horses parading proudly up and down the Ladies' Mile. 'That one's the grandest,' Lysette said, pointing to a high black stallion. 'No, I mean that one. Oh Tranby, look at the way that one shakes his tail!' she exclaimed, holding tightly to my arm and squealing like a joyful schoolgirl. Lysette's hair was piled high atop her head, caught up in a silk net decorated with tiny roses, and she wore a stunning pale pink ruffled dress with a huge back bustle that brushed against me as we walked. 'This is wonderful, Tranby,' she said, closing her eyes and drinking in the sun. 'It's strange, but when I'm with you, London seems more beautiful somehow.'

She wound her arms around me, and I hugged her in return; quickly, but none too ardently. I was afraid that if I held her too tight I might not let go, I might do something foolish which would embarrass us for ever. 'Wasn't that fine!' she said. 'And some day, we will be able to embrace freely, whenever and wherever we are seized with the feeling.'

'Yes,' I replied as I checked to see if anyone was watching while I clasped her hand. My mood darkened, and spies from the Institute suddenly seemed to spring up everywhere. 'Lysette, perhaps we should not appear together in public so frequently.'

'What do you mean?' she asked.

'Perhaps, and this is just an idea, mind you, but perhaps we should strive to demonstrate more restraint. Only in public, of course. What we do in private is another matter, but to the world we should display what Walt Whitman called "comrade love". At least that was what he called it among men. I'm not sure if a word exists for this kind of love among women. But we might do better to appear chaste. Even holy.'

'Oh. Perhaps you're right,' she said softly. 'I'm sorry if I've done something wrong.'

I began to envision a compromise that might bring me peace, a less frightening way to safely face the world. My steps quickened to match my tumbling thoughts and my black shawl fluttered behind me in the breeze. Lysette struggled to match my pace. 'We should give the appearance of a suffering love, a sacrificing love, not a sexual love. How much better this will seem! A secret love, by necessity, must be measured and marked by stolen kisses and half-held handshakes. A love with its ear always cocked towards the unlocked door,' I pronounced with finality.

We walked on quietly for a few yards and then she stopped. 'Tranby, what's happened? What's frightened you?' she began, carefully choosing her words.

'Nothing,' I answered, and it was almost the truth. My fear came from nothing, from a dream or a feeling, a midnight writing grasped from a dark corner of my brain and pushed to the forefront of everyday life. 'I dreamt that I left you. I left you alone,' I told her quickly, ashamed and embarrassed.

'But I don't believe you would ever do that. Not without good reason,' she insisted.

'I know,' I said. 'But, still, the thought frightened me.'

'Let's just sit and rest a bit,' Lysette suggested, leading me to a bench, where we sat down. She sighed, and the small webbed roses fanned against the side of her face. She leaned against my arm with all of her weight, but then she withdrew. 'Am I too close? Too close for public view?' she asked, stiffening slightly.

'No, it's fine to sit so near each other. At least for now. No one is watching,' I whispered, pulling her so close I could feel her breath on my neck, and the movement of her ribs against mine. I was overwhelmed with desire, aching to touch her and kiss her, to disappear inside her, to run my fingers through her carefully-dressed hair. The pressure of public restraint only served to heighten my longings, giving me the dizzy urge to pull off my clothing and dance freely through the streets.

We were quiet for a while. I did not speak for fear our brief time together would be shortened by the unnecessary expense of breath and thought and voices. In our compromise, even the air between us would be rarefied, something to be savoured, something to be treasured and kept. I patted her hand as coolly as I could, and fought off the urge to nuzzle her neck, to lift off the veil of pink netting and stroke the pale backs of her shoulders.

Children played around the benches, ignoring us unless an errant ball or bicycle passed our way, and then these children considered us only briefly as they retrieved the thing they loved. Grim-faced wetnurses in white caps and starched collars barrelled past us wheeling elaborate prams. No one looked at us for more than a moment, and I indulged in the foolish fantasy that we could truly disappear, disappear simply, without all the drama of actually running away.

Lysette was nearly asleep beside me, breathing deep and easy, when suddenly she sat forward with a start. 'Oh! Do you know what I dreamed last night? It was wonderful,' she said, pressing her chest.

'Tell me,' I insisted quickly. 'Let me steal your dreams and use them to replace my own.'

'I dreamed I was inside your heart.'

'Inside my heart? However did you end up there?' I asked.

Her eyebrows knitted together and her forehead wrinkled as she considered the question. 'I have no idea how I got there. You know how dreams are, they make perfect sense at night. Only in the morning do they seem impossible. In any event, your heart was beautiful. It was shaped like a temple, with red walls and high domes all around me, and I followed a winding path towards the middle, and there, in the centre of your heart, was a portrait of me! What a lovely surprise, to find the image of myself hidden inside your heart.'

She squeezed my hand and smiled, and I smiled too, until I thought about Jonnie, and how, if Lysette had seen my heart, she must surely have seen the scar left by that sad experience. 'I have doubts, Lysette. Sometimes I fear that my heart is lacking in something. Some vital element or segment that prevents me from loving as I'd like to. That prevents me from giving you everything you deserve,' I told her.

'Shh,' she said, stroking my hand. 'You mustn't believe that. I love you, Tranby, just as you are. My brilliant instructor. When you lecture to the class, you look so serious and stern, but then I see you smile, only at me, and I can see what no one else can, I can see what you are thinking.'

'Lysette, do you know where I would like to take you some day? To see the temple of the Inca god in Cuzco. The temple is huge, and the inner walls are encrusted with gold and silver and emeralds in a giant effigy of the sun, so when the real sun rises, the light through the doorway hits the wall and the false sun appears to burst into flames! If only I could see such a sight, if only I could gaze on such a wonder,' I said, squeezing Lysette's hand. I felt myself near tears as I considered all the beauty of the world which I feared my eyes would never behold. 'Wouldn't that be breath-taking?' Sorrow rose in my throat as I felt the dull earth spin slowly beneath my feet, carrying adventures further and further out of my reach.

Lysette relaxed beside me. 'Yes,' she admitted. 'It sounds

very beautiful. But not as lovely as the inside of your heart. I still think that would be the better adventure.'

A gentle hour passed and she stirred and stretched as the sun dipped behind the clouds. We both knew it was time for her to catch her train home. She stood stiffly, and I moved to help her.

'Don't,' she said softly, lifting a hand and pressing me back to the bench. 'Let me leave you now, and walk away as if we don't mean so very much to each other. Remember, we must beware of who may see us leaving.'

I nodded my head. Tears collected in my throat but I said nothing. This was for the best. We had to behave with a lesser show of public emotion, and the more we practised, the easier it would be. We had to display the hallmarks of true English gentlewomen: modesty, service, and forgetfulness of self.

Lysette pressed her hands into the small of her back as her hips pushed forward. She sighed and found her balance before taking a few tentative steps down the pathway, using her parasol as a kind of walking stick. Her steps quickened and I watched her move out of my world and towards her other life, the public life of which I took no part. She was a kind of night star, returning now to shed light on her husband's masculine planet; forsaking my world, and leaving it barren and cold.

'Wait,' I called out suddenly, surprising myself at the vigour in my voice. 'Wait just one moment. Let me at least walk you as far as the station. Surely no harm can come from that.' I caught up to her quickly and she said nothing. I thought at first she might be angry, but when we linked arms, I caught the tail-end of her brilliant smile, and it was as dazzling as a comet, as vibrant as a shooting star.

'Why do I endure you, Tranby Quirke?' she asked and laughed. 'I imagine it is because I love you so much.'

By the time we reached the station, the weather had changed, and the cooler afternoon sky was now as blue as painted Dutch plates. The people waiting for trains were pink-cheeked and impatient as we moved among them, but were not touched by them. The platforms were crowded with tall women and round-faced men who watched passively while their happy children, overdressed in caps and smocks and bonnets, played with gaily coloured wooden toys.

When we found the platform for the train to Hampstead, Lysette suddenly pulled out of her pocket a small bag of chocolates and sweetmeats and held it in her fist. 'I bought these for you at Harrods,' she said. 'I told Malcolm I was buying him some handkerchiefs. It isn't much, just a little something. So you can think of me after I've gone.' As I looked at the lop-sided net bag tied with shiny pink ribbon, Lysette's words filled me with melancholy and remorse. I thought I might have preferred to leave without saying good-bye to her; leaving her this way felt like a type of little death, a death by inches, by pieces, by whimper and by cry.

Lysette's eyes widened and her face flushed. 'Don't be sad, Tranby,' she said. 'This present was supposed to make you smile.' She offered me the sweets and tried to hide her disappointment with a false smile that narrowed her plush lips and pulled at the sides of her face. 'Now remember not to eat them all at once, you'll have a stomach pain,' she warned. I smiled sadly and took her hand, unable to find any voice within the empty depths of my chest.

'I can't bear the thought of not seeing you until next week,' she scolded me. She reached to touch my cheek but stopped just before her fingers met my skin. 'Tell me how I'm expected to survive the rest of my life like this, Love.'

I shook my head, knowing that no words of explanation existed. I took the bag of sweets.

'Oh Lysette, thank you for this,' I said softly. 'I'm sure they will taste wonderful.' Lysette didn't understand the essence of my sorrow; she didn't know how far I felt from hunger now. We slid into a tender embrace and she cried as she held me close. My chin touched her collarbone as I tried to comfort her by stroking her trembling shoulder. 'It's all right,' I said, indulging in the lie. 'It's all right. The days pass quickly,' but as I said the words, I felt a stutter that slowed the motion of my heart.

'But it hurts to let you go,' she whispered in my ear.

'It hurts me too,' I said, squeezing her more tightly in my arms. I wished I could press her into my chest. I wanted to fashion her into another heart for myself and carry her with me wherever I might go. I wanted her always to be moving inside me, I wanted to feel her even in sleep. I wanted to hear her as a soft rumble under my ribs, and be aware of a hum in my side when I turned over in the night.

Lysette stepped back slightly and her hands played absently at my collar as she tried to pull the sides of my shawl together over my throat. 'You'll catch a death of chill,' she scolded. Her gestures were the more tender for being unnecessary. I held her hands but I couldn't grab her face, not there on the platform, not where everyone was watching us, sharing handshakes and pouring on and off wooden platforms that rumbled and quaked with every approaching train.

We might have been mistaken for nothing more than friends, but her beauty would have raised questions in a few alert minds. Sisters perhaps, or maybe even cousins; a few tender embraces between us might have passed unnoticed, but what I really wanted to do to her, right there, right then, would have landed us in Holloway Prison. Desire licked at my hollow insides. I shivered, but not from the cold. I ached to taste the inside of her folded, generous, mysterious lip. Heat rose in waves up the back of my neck and I simply wanted to press and press and press against her until there was nothing left of either of us. She squeezed my hand and I knew she felt the same way. She looked down at me and passed the tip of her tongue tightly around her lip and gave small dry kisses to a little spot carved into the air.

'What a sorry life,' I told her. 'A world where we can never be honest in public.'

'I know,' she sighed. 'A sorry life. But less sorry now. Malcolm made me desolate. You give me hope. To have you and me, Tranby and Lysette, together in this life is enough.' She pulled back a little and centred me in her green-eyed gaze. Then she opened my shawl and slipped her hand inside my dress, pressing her palm against my breast. 'Keep me right here,' she ordered, as what remained of my body melted into a luminous pool. I winced. 'Does that hurt?' she asked, as her hand arched and stiffened.

'No,' I said. 'It isn't that.'

'You feel cold.' She sighed, and a membrane vibrated inside me. Hair stood up on the back of my neck.

'Not now. Not any more. You fill me up. You make me complete.' I wished her hand would have stayed there for ever. I began to feel warm and safe, protected from the chilling wind that moments earlier blew right through me. Suddenly a man jostled us, pushing past with a suitcase, and Lysette's hand slid out of my dress front. I began to weep.

'Good Lord no, what have I done?' Lysette said as she pulled out her white handkerchief and held it to my face.

'You've made me fall in love with you,' I said as I struggled to compose myself. No one had seen this happen, as the twenty-seven past four to Hampstead via Marylebone barrelled in behind us, and now she was huddled very close to my chest. I wrapped my arm around her and our foreheads touched, sizzling where skin met skin. I dared not go any further. She took my hand again and I watched her tremble, seeing the sparks in her eyes and the slight fissures rising in her fierce brave face. I smiled sadly and she looked away.

'That's my train. It's waiting. But before I go, remind me again of the things that haven't gone wrong for us,' she asked earnestly. 'Tell me you believe we are lucky.'

'I can't think of anything to say,' I told her. 'No, that's a lie, I can think of some things, but I won't name them aloud. The longer I think, the longer I can stay here with you.'

She nodded gently and we were silent as we lingered, pressed into an embrace, waiting as if we had all the time in the world, as if Lysette's train was not already waiting for her just over our shoulders. We lingered the way lovers linger, with our fingers falling endlessly over each other, brushing lips and chins and necks; teasing the taut nerve endings that dared to remember every texture, made each gesture an event.

I was just inches from kissing her lips when a huge and looming figure, bearing down the platform, jumped suddenly into view. 'Move away!' I whispered to Lysette. She stood motionless. 'I say do it, move away, now!' Still she did not move, so with the palm of my hand, just the palm, flat and firm, I pushed her into the crowd behind me, and she was momentarily invisible among the many high-hatted, swirling-skirted, beribboned, giggling women, as Miss Wilhelmina Fickle herself, off-balance with gift boxes, lumbered through the crowd. She pushed people out of her way, left and right, and I tried to duck out of her line of sight; wishing, hoping, I could be instantly invisible, that I could blink my eyes and disappear.

'Miss Quirke! Miss Quirke!' Her unmistakable voice boomed over the chatter of the crowd. 'Do wait for me, Miss Quirke!' It was no use trying to escape now. I had no choice but to face her. Meanwhile, another train pulled into the station and the crowd thinned as people piled aboard. The jostling of the crowd pushed Lysette forward again until she was just behind me, at my side. Lysette reached out to touch me, but I drew my arm away.

'I should say, Miss Quirke, what a pleasant surprise to see you out and about on such a lovely afternoon,' Miss Fickle panted as she put down her shopping. She pulled a handkerchief out of her pocket and mopped her damp, florid brow, fanning her face and waiting to catch her breath. 'I was under the impression that you spent all your free time reading maps and writing articles,' she continued with a tone of affected surprise. Her gaze slipped away from my face and landed squarely on Lysette. Miss Fickle's neck reddened and her pupils widened with excitement as her mind made the connection. 'And this is your young pupil here, is it not? Indeed, I believe it is. I know you are a devoted teacher, Miss Quirke, but I hardly realised that weekend shopping excursions counted as part of your lesson plan. Or is it only certain students who are offered the opportunity for,' she paused, 'social advancement?'

'No!' I said quickly. 'This is not what you think it is.' I laughed nervously. 'Mrs McDonald here, my student . . . yes, she is my student of course, but we were not shopping together. No no no. What a silly thing to presume! I was on my way to pick up a book I had ordered from a shop in Oxford Street, and she was, I can't remember, but she did tell me where she was going . . . she was shopping for something for her husband, that was it, and we happened to see each other near Speaker's Corner. Well, I didn't see any harm in inviting her for a cup of tea, as I would have invited any student whom I happened to meet unexpectedly . . .' My mind turned frantically as my voice trailed away. I wanted to erase myself from the earth, I wanted the ground to open up and swallow me whole. Suddenly I remembered the sweets in my hand. The net bag felt damp and sticky and I was seized with the desire to throw it under the wheels of the train. I shoved it under a fold of my shawl, afraid Miss Fickle had noticed it and recognised it as a gift from Lysette, proof that there was something private between us.

A whistle blew over my shoulder. 'That's my train,' Miss Fickle announced, swooping down and grabbing the handles of her shopping bags. 'Sorry I can't stay and chat, but I shall speak to you Monday morning,' she said ominously as she waddled away and hoisted herself heavily on to the train across from us.

That train immediately chugged away, seething and straining and belching black smoke, seemingly belaboured by the weight of Miss Fickle, who was probably settling heavily into her seat. My face burned with shame and I was afraid to look back at Lysette, standing still and silent, directly over my shoulder.

'I'm sorry for what I've just done,' I told her. 'I wouldn't blame you if you couldn't forgive me.'

She didn't say anything, and as I slowly turned towards her, I could perceive no movement in her body, not even a breath in her chest. It was as if she had been struck suddenly to stone. 'Lysette?' I asked. 'Please say something. Anything.'

I looked up. Lysette's face appeared strange and spotty, shocked to the point she could barely speak. Her eyes were enormous, but her pupils were tiny black pinpoints of glowing hot coal. Her face trembled, but the rest of her body was still. 'I will take the pain which I feel at this moment,' she said slowly, gulping out the words, 'as proof of how much I must love you. I did not think anything could hurt me so much.'

'I'm sorry, but I was afraid she might inform the Board of Governors, and I would be relieved of my position . . .'

She interrupted. 'No, Tranby. That isn't it. The truth is that you are ashamed. Ashamed of me.' At that her hand flew to her mouth as she choked out a few sobs.

I felt horrified. 'Not ashamed of you, Lysette, ashamed of me. Not you, me.' I reached out to take her arm, but she turned and began to walk away, quickly at first, but after a few steps her gait slowed. I knew, somehow, that she was waiting for me. She was asking me to follow her, she wanted me to run after her, to apologise and explain, to grab her in my arms and kiss her and tell her it had all been a terrible mistake. It was not too late; she was offering me the chance to have her back, and more than anything in the world I was prepared to do that, to do anything to redeem the damage I had done. But just as I took a step forward, I was struck by a tearing sensation in my chest. I caught my breath and the pain jagged through me, from my neck all the way down deep into my stomach. I felt dizzy and light-headed, and Lysette, still not too far in front of me, disappeared into a blur of jumping colour. I blinked and blinked but could not pick out her image in the rushing whirl. It felt as if a great bird had his talons in my chest, grasping and plucking, pulling me to shreds, and I staggered to a bench at the edge of the platform. I sank down, leaning forward with my arms around my knees. I had the giddy hope that I might die, and never be faced with the pain of what I'd done. I sat for several minutes, wheezing and gulping for air, watching the world around me spin and turn.

When I was able to breathe again, my eyesight steadied. The station was nearly empty. There was no sign of Lysette anywhere, and I imagined her on the train, sitting near the window, but I darkened the part of my mind that noticed she was stiff-shouldered and weeping, explaining to the woman beside her about the cinder in her eye, the tiny thing which caused her to weep such ferocious and copious tears. I drew the shade against my soul, barred the door to sorrow. The pain in my chest had passed completely, and I felt nothing but a settled emptiness; a vague, familiar dullness that spread from the centre of my soul through to the ends of my finger-tips; a radiating silence which did not have enough depth to be considered sadness, nor enough weight to call it grief. I was so bereft of form and structure that as I stood, I felt I might just as well have floated home.

I left the station and followed the slowest road south, walking all the way; covering so many miles that my feet wept and bled, but I found comfort in the dull rhythm of step after step. I opened the bag of sweets and ate them slowly. My jaw ached as the chocolates melted, bleeding their black juices over my tongue, and I savoured each one like a kiss. I let each piece dissolve and be swallowed like a stream of sugary tears.

Lysette Lysette Lysette— I whispered her name. In my mind's eye I saw the pink back of her hat as she skirted down the Hyde Park pathway. At Lavender Hill I could still see that image, even as the cottages gave way to tenement blocks, and the shiny windows changed places with the hollow shells of buildings stained by lamp black and decay. Even in those dark teeming streets where rats quibbled in doorways and flogged horses stumbled before their carts, I could see her; through the shadowed alleys, my path was lit by her comet-bright smile.

I still heard her voice, heard the music of her accent, the descending crescents of her speech. Even the sound of factory wheels and textile mills belching black smoke did not erase her voice, or her whisper tickling my ear.

Her kiss, her kiss, I had to find her last kiss! I fell to the ground and began searching for some proof that she had once loved me.

'Madam, can I help you?' a voice called above me. I looked up into the face of an older gentleman whose white hair and yellowy eyes were bright with kindness. 'Have you by chance lost something?' he asked.

'Yes,' I said. 'Something so valuable, more valuable than gold.'

'Well then, do let me help you find it,' the man offered. 'Could you describe this object you've lost?'

How could I explain to this stranger the shape, weight, and characteristics of Lysette's last kiss? 'Thank you for your kind offer,' I told the stranger, 'but this is something so small, so strange and precious that only I can see it.' And so he doffed his hat, bowed, and continued onwards. That initial kiss, no more substantial than the brush of butterfly wings, that kiss so quickly and thoughtlessly bestowed when we greeted one another just inside the Hyde Park gate – How could I have known that would be the last kiss ever? Had it soaked into my skin; had I brushed it away with the back of my hand?

I stood and continued towards home. I knew the kiss was lost well before I reached the railway tracks and trekked across the open scrub fields. I saw no sign of that kiss in the old fields of dying artichokes and wild asparagus, or in the camp of caravanning gypsies, who had settled in until Christmas with their goats and carts and mourning, sad-faced donkeys.

Lysette's scent, delicate and elusive, still filled my nose as it fought with the stench of carbon, plumbago, and coal dust. Even the fumes from the oil refineries could not obscure Lysette's essence of lavender and lemon oil. As I worked my way down Coldharbour Lane, oppressive with the stench of dogs and coal fires and overworked horses, a breath of wind stirred up Lysette's scent until it grew to the density of smoke before it settled, nearly imperceptible, again. Her scent lived in the soil, in the elements that came alive at night, in the odours that stirred the fading flowers into budding once more.

I reached Camberwell and stopped briefly outside the bakery. Through the front window I could see Mrs Hambleton sitting near the ovens. She had given birth a week earlier and was clasping the small, bald child to her breast. Most likely she chose to feed him near the ovens because that was the warmest and least draughty spot in the building. He, for I had heard it was a boy, was a weak and sickly baby and not given much chance for survival. But Mrs Hambleton managed to look both resigned and resolute, and I admired her courage. She rocked back and forth impassively, but she held her jaw firmly, and her face was hardened by hope.

I looked up at the warped wooden sign above me, 'Hambleton's Bakery Shop', which hung limply on its chain and creaked and sighed helplessly, a hostage to the rattling wind. I remembered that when I had left home that morning, it was with the thought that I might never return.

I wound my way up the narrow steel staircase, breathing in the scent of babies, yeast, and boiled milk, of baker's sweat and good hard bread; those solid, homely smells which I hoped would fill the emptiness inside me. But once I opened my door, Lysette's spirit began to torment me. She was with me while I bathed and ate and read, and the more I tried to avoid her, the larger she loomed, and when I lay down to sleep I saw her weeping, and then I wept myself. Lysette made my dreams so vivid and so enchanting that I woke the next morning with an ache in my head like a dying gaslight. The pain ebbed and lessened over time, until by sundown I was released from this vision, but then, just as a wise monster once promised, I cried to dream again.

CHAPTER SEVEN

My darling Lysette – I am in exile in the most barren and desolate place on the earth, a land of perpetual winter, an Arctic zone so cold it sears the skin like an opposite sun. Believe me when I say that never have I felt so completely silent. So far from you, and yet so near; your image always with me, painted gaily on my eyelid's inner side. If I possessed a heart, it would be beating very slowly, and if my face were visible to living eyes, it would appear quiet and mysterious, heavy-lidded and in a position of gentle repose. At last I feel protected, in a place where the Pole itself is magnetic, and helps me to hide by sending contradictory messages to the world, confusing compasses, and sending ordinary instruments spinning.

I warm myself over a flame fed by oily walrus blubber and I meditate on my inability to love. But what good is my regret now, when I am exiled to this frozen landscape where you share my dreams with manatees, the strange 40-foot long ladies of the frozen sea, who look like animals above the navel, and suspiciously like fish below.

It is August now, and already winter is rushing in around me, sweeping across the broad white plains of Franz Josef Land. I dream of the Augusts below the Arctic Circle, and see the sweet Norwegian cherries in their fatted prime on the deep and clean fjords. I will survive the winter. I eat well and my stomach is never empty. Not for me the pain of scurvy, the swollen hands and feet, the dying fingers and the toothless, blackened gums. I dine on bear meat soup for breakfast, fried bear steaks for lunch, and finish off with duck egg omelettes afterwards, thick and triple-yolked. My stomach is full and only my heart remains empty.

The silence here, Lysette, is so complete that if you could sit beside me, we would hear the blood fluttering in each other's ears, and it would sound as soft as butterflies. And when I turn to kiss you, the warmth of our kiss would crack our cold lips and shame the snow into melting. We could watch the rows of icicles flash and glitter like defiant lovers, shining with all the bright certainty of suicide blades. We could be two snowflakes and rest here unmolested, like spring blossoms hidden in the hard-packed icy earth.

I leave my hut and wander outside, into a thin atmosphere barren, beautiful, and deceptively deadly. Ghosts live here, preserved in the rare polar air as firmly as pickled ginger stalks floating eerily in a clear glass jar. Sir John Franklin himself seems to look down from the invisible bows of his two doomed ships, *Erebus* and *Terror*, as he whips up ice storms to match his tantrums and his bluer moods. Every fierce wind carries the memory of Vitus Bering, battling the vicious Siberian Chucki and still searching for his Gamaland, somewhere off the frozen coast of Kamchatka.

My feet slide cleanly against the ice, moving as smoothly as glass against glass. I let my eyes glaze over as my thoughts return to you, Lysette. My tears are only briefly liquid; they freeze while falling and shatter as they strike the ground.

I wish more than anything I could bundle up beside you, curl up in a polar bear pelt and hold your body close to my own. I want to let my breath warm and redden your freezing cheek. The wind will cloud my sun-defying spectacles, so you slide them off my face and hide them in your pocket. 'You're cold as well,' you say, and smile at that memory, then gently press your hands to my forehead and your touch warms the empty sockets of my eyes.

I blink and your image disappears. I am surrounded by nothing but snow and ice and a thin high milky sky. 'I love you, Lysette,' I shout as I have never shouted before, and the sky seems to crack open above me, perhaps because the air is thinner here at the top of the world, or perhaps because the earth itself is surprised to hear me say the words so freely. 'I miss you, my darling Lysette, and I love you more than life itself.'

It came as little surprise to me when Lysette no longer attended my class on *Popular Thought for Modern Women*. Her empty desk, second row, third from the left, took on the dimensions of a lopsided emptiness, a gaping and unbalanced sadness that constantly reshaped itself to the new demands of grief and pain and self-recrimination; a twice-weekly reminder of the precious thing I had given away.

With the balance of my soul, I missed Lysette desperately. I longed to capture her and beg her to accept my apologies and return to my life. I wondered what Henry Stanley might have done in this situation; Stanley that great Bula Matari, that breaker of rocks? Or Captain Cook? Or the taciturn but determined Vitus Bering? They would have set sail to retrieve her, of course. They would have called out a fleet of their strongest and most sea-worthy vessels, sailed forever, fed off leather and rope, and not stopped even for fresh water until they had sighted her horizon.

But I did no such thing. No. Not Tranby Quirke. I closed my soul. I hid my feelings, stashed them back inside my chest, into the hollow cave that remembered their dimensions. I no longer cut fresh flowers, and I fasted at least three times a week, until even the dark shadows between my ribs cast darker shadows on the ribs beneath. I visited the spinsters and hauled soup like a martyr. I returned to my WSPU meetings and kept detailed minutes of each and every tedious debate. I helped devise several new suffrage slogans – *Life Is Female*, *The World Is Female First*, and *The Suffering Of The World Is Borne By The Female Body* were among the best; and while my sisters heckled every Liberal Party candidate within reach, waving white banners and roaring the war cry of 'Will You Give Votes For Women?', I stood in the background as usual, collecting overcoats and distributing biscuits. I drank tea, more tea than was probably healthy for me; so much tea in fact that my hands shook and my stomach churned, even while I engaged in acts otherwise unlikely to excite my blood. I made frequent visits to my parents' graves in Peckham Cemetery, the only spot in England where I could weep freely, where I could hurl my body to the earth and feel the pebbles press against my skin; the only place where my grief gave rise to no questions.

And I adjusted, although it shames me to admit it now; adjusted in the little ways one learns to adapt to loss or grief or disappointment. My heart, like a sun, blazed brightly for a time, but now it had been eclipsed again and slid back into its deep black shadow. My spirit dipped and slumbered, and something about that fact felt strangely correct. I experienced none of the dizzying symptoms of love; no dancing nerves, no quivering heart, no trembling knees. A peaceful lack of feeling settled over me. I was the old Tranby Quirke again, the woman who could not love, and I discovered that the sands of the soul settle eventually; they level out and learn to rest, even begin collecting dust.

On 16 September, four days ago now, Agnes Ellington-Pilch passed away after what appeared to have been a life, a last illness, and a death marked by modesty, grace, and decorum. She left this earth surrounded by the things she loved: her books, her Belgian linen, her fine bone china. She owed nothing, and was owed nothing, her papers were in order, her bills paid, her notes filed, and her beloved Hotspur packed off to a good home. Sarah Robbins and I were with Agnes at the end, and she went peacefully, sighing and settling into the bedsheets as she relinquished her battle and gave up the ghost.

Twenty minutes earlier she had spoken her last words, in the same firm, determined voice which had reprimanded me for my poor poetry reading. 'Janet,' she had said, 'Janet, come here, dear, step into the light. Janet, at last you may safely take my hand.'

As Agnes spoke those words, a gentle melancholy enveloped me, settling at the edges of my heart. I was touched by the tender memory of her childhood friend. 'Well, perhaps Agnes and Janet will meet again in the next world,' I said softly to Sarah as she laid down her prayer book and blew out the last candles that had so solemnly graced the bedside table.

'That seems rather unlikely,' Sarah replied. 'Lady Janet is still alive. Alive and well and living in Chelsea.'

'Is she?' I asked, surprised. 'Well then, why wasn't she told of Agnes' illness? Would she not have wanted to visit her dear old friend?'

'Didn't you know?' Sarah asked conspiratorially, in a voice impolitely loud for a room in which a well-respected woman had so recently died. 'There was a scandal, many years ago. In Italy. Agnes nearly drowned, but Lady Janet plunged into the sea and rescued her. But then as Agnes recovered from the accident, it came to light that she and Lady Janet were, well, they were, unnatural friends. You know, they were lesbians.' The word sounded harsh and sibilant, rushing through the room like an unwelcome wind. 'When their families found out, they were furious. Lord Somerville forbade them to see each other ever again, and then he pushed Lady Janet into that quick marriage with Sir Hugh.' Sarah rolled her eyes, nearly breathless with excitement. 'Would you ever have believed it? Agnes Ellington-Pilch, one of the most highly regarded women of our time!'

'I don't know,' I said softly, looking down at the tiny, crab-like figure which lay breathless beneath the sheets and beyond all sorrow now. 'Perhaps I could have believed it. Perhaps I could.'

I was numb for the first few hours after Agnes' death. The dullness I had felt since my betrayal of Lysette seemed to protect me from grief, serving as a sort of casing of cotton-wool between myself and the rest of the world. But as I lay in bed that night I could not sleep, my mind so troubled by frightening dreams. I began to review Agnes' life in light of this new information – that she had been an invert, like myself and, like me, had lived a hidden life and, like me, had turned away from the one she truly loved. Now I saw why she chose me as her successor. She had been much more my friend than I had ever realised, and perhaps, had I been more honest with her, she might have confided in me everything.

How cold Agnes must be now, I suddenly thought, and I could not endure the image – poor Agnes, so cold and damp in the dark rich earth, finally able to weep freely. How I longed to reach her now, and apologise for the comfort and kindness I withheld. How cold she must be – no, wait a moment, not cold, for now she is free; how cold she must have been then, during those evenings when I visited her in her immaculate flat, with her china teapot, her Belgian lace, and her leather-bound poetry. She had been surrounded by her favourite things and yet utterly alone, with only a dim memory of Lady Janet beating inside her brain, a memory longing to be set free, but she would not breach her silence. Not even to me; her hand-picked successor, and even I could not be told.

I began to imagine all the conversations we might have had, sitting close together by her fire with a blanket round our shoulders, drinking tea and sharing memories. I would have told her about Jonnie, and she would have nodded sadly, thinking about the drowned girl, and commenting on how she had nearly become the drowned girl in someone else's heart, but she had been saved. We would have spoken honestly about the beauty of women, and the wild emotions they sometimes engendered, and what it was like, as an invert, to feel so odd, so stricken by strangeness, and yet so deeply wonderful, both at the same time. She would have known and understood all those feelings, and neither one of us need have felt lonely.

I delved deeper into my bed, trying to escape the chill silence that swept into my head. 'But I've done good things,' I protested to the walls around me, and in the echo I heard how tiny and feeble my little voice sounded. The room was so cold; everything felt cold and hollow. I had let everything reduce itself to this. Only Lysette mattered, and I had given her away. *Like the base Indian, threw a pearl away, richer than all his tribe . . .*

I wanted to disappear. I was barely more than a spectre anyway, how much more difficult to die? It seemed to me I had died already; four weeks and two days ago, when I betrayed Lysette and I had been too weak-willed even to accept what I had done. My life was like a ship that had set sail long ago, and what little passed for feeling in me was like a ship's light blinking in the distance, reaching shore only long after the flame had gone out.

My mind spun backwards, hurtling through the years. When had I let this happen? When had I let go of life? I settled on that midnight carriage ride to London – it had to have happened then. The whisper in the wheels, the voice of bats and owls above us, and the thudding of my lungs and bones – it was not death we fled that night, but life. *Fly life, Tranby, fly life.* Run as far and as fast as you can from the truth of who you are. That is precisely what I have done for twenty-two years, and my bitter victory is that I have at last succeeded. I have succeeded in escaping life itself. The carriage ride is over, and finally, I may lay my body down to rest. Yes. Rest. At last.

Yesterday afternoon Agnes Ellington-Pilch was buried in Highgate Cemetery, sentenced to spend for ever beside the brief husband she could never abide in life. I watched from just inside the cemetery gates as they sank that casket in the pit of the damp autumn earth, and I felt the echo in the pit of my heart, as if her body, in dropping, carried with it the bitter residue of my own deeply hidden dreams.

'Rest, Agnes, rest. Do not be afraid of the cold and the damp. You are dear to someone, and I will join you soon,' I whispered. The two dozen mourners who were on hand kept careful control over their emotions, in respect of Agnes' wishes, which had included a request for no vulgar shows of grief. A few attendants dabbed tears or covered reddened noses, but I was the only one to weep outright, to weep freely. Through the funeral of Agnes Ellington-Pilch I saw my own end. No six bells would ring out to mark my passing. The few mourners at my funeral would no doubt be professional mutes, hired to stand about the grim little churchyard and lend the ceremony an air of solemnity, and of dignity, of which I deserved none. I could see my thin, pale, hollow body, as dry and bloodless as a South American insect captured under glass, gathering dust in my flat until eventually discovered by the suspicious Miss Fickle, who would alert the Simperton Institute to cancel my classes. Someone, it made no difference who, would surely return my borrowed library books, suspend my order with the cabinet makers in Bethnal Green, and drop a brief note to the Playgoers' Society of Penge, explaining my recent absences, and returning my tickets to next season's social readings of *Euripides* and *Oedipus Rex*.

'Agnes Ellington-Pilch was certainly a grand lady,' I overheard Mrs Stevens say to her husband as the mourners dispersed, flitting quickly from the churchyard like a flock of black-clad birds.

'Indeed she was. A tribute to British womanhood,' Mr Stevens concurred. 'An inspiration to us all.'

If only you knew the truth. None of you knew her; the true Agnes, the invisible woman. All the love and pain and sorrow, buried inside her all these years, a secret within a secret, and all buried now. Agnes swallowed the truth the way the earth will swallow her, and she will decay the way her love did – dying. Drying. Slowly, silently turning to dust on her tongue. Returning to the earth she came from, her body hardly different from the elements around it, with no proof that any of it ever . . . was. Now she lay quiet in the cold, cold ground; alone, and inconsolable. But not for long, for I will join her soon, I will close my arms around her, I will comfort her and keep her warm.

I excused myself from the queue of mourners, who were drifting from the churchyard, scattering into carriages and hansom cabs. Their thoughts had already shifted; I could see the changes in their eyes and their hands and in their slackening features. The funeral had ended, they had paid their respects, and now it was time to think of food and tea, and the evening's entertainment; perhaps an opera, or a revue at the Empire or the Alhambra, and a glass of sherry afterwards, sitting by the fireplace with a good cigar . . . I ran back to the grave site and fell to my knees, burying my face in the black softness of my shawl. I longed to reach into the ground, take Agnes' hand and find renewed life flowing warmly through her fingers. I began to recite her poem, speaking with all the feeling I could muster. '*And bless thee, for thy lips are bland, And bright the friendship of thine eye, And in my thoughts with scarce a sigh, I take the pressure of thine hand . . .*'

Once I had had my fill of grieving, I returned to my flat, where a tall stack of my students' assignments sat on my desk, waiting patiently for the corrections which now would never come. I closed the door carefully and turned the key, and the very silence of the empty room seemed to find an echo somewhere deep inside my body, inside my hollow chest. I gazed at my mantelpiece, where the little net bag sat like a silent memorial, keeping steadfast watch. That last gift from Lysette, empty now but still tied with the shining pink ribbon, remembered grief, and kept the shape of what was once inside it. I picked up the bag and held it gently in the palm of my hand.

I could feel myself fading. Fading. Fading fast. *Miss Tranby Quirke, aged 34 years, of Camberwell, died today.* Funny, we all thought she died long ago. And then I heard another voice, tapping my shoulders and offering me release from sorrow: *Repair thou to me with as much speed as thou wouldest fly life. Fly life, Tranby, fly life . . .*

CHAPTER EIGHT

Four hours ago I swallowed a bitter cup of hot black Chinese tea, a drink which included a pinch of arsenic, the juice of two suspicious mushrooms, a tablespoon of powdered soap, and a few drops of fragrant nectar squeezed from the blades of a weepy azalea. Then I sat down to write this story, and I can say with certainty, at a few minutes before seven o'clock, that death comes to me with gentle comfort; a sweet warm certainty that rises in my veins. I feel the poison working on me as I sit here now; slowing my blood, stiffening my limbs, and creeping up behind me like a man in a long black cape, ready to rise up and cast his shadow.

The irony of this obscure death is not lost on me. I had once, so long ago that I barely remember it now, dreamed of possessing the spirit of some great explorer, perhaps even the soul of Prince Henry himself, the fifteenth-century Portuguese royal whose horoscope was said to have destined him to 'toil at high and mighty conquests, especially in seeking out things that were hidden from other men'. That might have been me, I believed; all I had needed was the right opportunity. I once lived with the hope of discovering some great, important, valuable thing.

But not now. Now I'll fade away quietly into that grey, impalpable place, and no one will wet the earth with tears for my passing. No one will publicly proclaim my virtues, I will receive no eulogy like Captain Cook, whom King George III praised as the perfect explorer, a gentleman by his manners, and blessed with a body not prone to illness, a brain designed for calculations, and a viscera which could stomach dog meat, sea lions, and fresh kangaroo.

And I think also of David Livingstone, who died in 1873; alone, yes, but not without his devoted servants, Susi and Chuma, who, following his final wishes, cut out his heart and buried it in the African earth, and wept many tears over the darkened soil; those two who loved him so dearly they dried his body in the sunshine and afterwards sewed him into a long white length of sailcloth, and carried him on their shoulders more than 1,000 miles to the African coast, and unable even then to bid him good-bye, they carried him aboard the ship to Zanzibar, and kept watch over his body on the journey towards England, and never left his side until he was put to his final rest inside the cool stony caverns of Westminster Abbey, where they could turn away from his death and begin comforting each other.

I look around me and try to derive some satisfaction from the little, silly, shallow things; my dresser, the bed, the Viennese shelves. My cats sleep peacefully at the side of the fireplace. They twitch when the ashes crackle; then they stretch and settle back into themselves, oblivious to my dismal scene. I can hear the Hambleton children beneath me, kicking against the walls; their tiny feet beat out a rhythm to their restlessness, to their crowded, three-to-a-bed dreams. The newest Hambleton baby, born into this sad world six weeks ago, cries inconsolably. Perhaps he mourns the spirit world he left behind, the spirit world which, just now, opens its doors and beckons me in.

A last phrase trickles through my brain: *like the base Indian, threw a pearl away, richer than all his tribe . . .* Shakespeare at my elbow, and when I least expect him. Did my father find this too, in his last moments of life? Was he surprised to find there was something more than poetry? I remember him on his deathbed, stern-faced and trembling, but he would not let me share his fear or grief. Although outwardly silent, inside I was screaming, 'Please, Father, please let me in; this is your last chance, please let me in . . .'

Or maybe the rhythm soothes me; perhaps it is the steady metre of the verse which plays the part of Lady Janet's powerful arm, and keeps me safe above the waves. *Richer than all his tribe, richer than all his tribe.* I close my eyes and rest my head upon my desk. My students' papers drop to the floor one by one, and my teaching seems not to have mattered for much at all. The world seems to slip away beneath me, spinning and draining beneath my feet. 'Richer than all his tribe,' finds a reply in the gentle settling of my blood.

Lysette, I'm sorry I could not love you better. May this fault be rectified by my death. I love you, I love you, I love you, Lysette.

PART FOUR

'In my heart's core, ay, in my heart of heart . . .'

Hamlet

CHAPTER NINE

My darling Lysette – I have found the strangest and most magnificent adventure, and it is much closer to home than I ever imagined. How could I have guessed that such wonders lived beneath my own skin? My spirit had left its shell, floating briefly above my body, and I might have been free then, free for ever from the confines of my life, but I had the urge to look behind me, to glance back and investigate the place that had failed me, so I slipped down again and burrowed back into my body, entering it as a stranger, expecting to tour an arid room, and capture the last breath of a dying organ before it gave up and stopped completely.

But what a surprise to see how beautiful the body is inside! I struggle to make a few notes, and my hand moves in time to the steady hum of blood. The throat is golden; clear, and smooth. The stomach lies flat; black, shiny, and nestled between tipped yellow kidneys. The stomach itself is not an appealing organ, but as I peer closer, I can see the dormant butterflies folded up inside, ready to flutter when I rise, splash water on my face and think of love.

I am moving into the bone marrow now. I know I must hurry, but I dare not miss a thing. The weight of the angels massing outside pushes me onwards. I can hear them whispering from where they sit and rock, perched atop the sternum. I heed their warning and burrow further inwards.

With a hiss I push myself up under a lung, and rest a moment, to catch my breath. A muscle twitches, and I know this is a sign that I must move quickly. I must make a pass at my quarry now, or lose the chance for ever. I jump on to the cresting wave of blood and ride it to its source, disembarking at the forefront to the heart.

I approach slowly, trying not to be overwhelmed. But I find that all my readings in anatomy have not prepared me for the heart's strange majesty.

—*No, Tranby, you must be scientific about it. Like Father taught you. Remember when he cut open the frog and showed you how the creature worked?*

Yes, and I was fascinated, true, but also disappointed, to see so much mystery suddenly explained.

All right then; Miss Tranby Quirke, scientist and famed explorer, submit your report:

The heart is small, rounded, lop-sided. One side appears larger than the other. It is not a pretty thing with its thick valves and pulsing arteries. Like a fleshy package, it appears to be tied in a knot at the top. I move forward cautiously, fearing both its obvious power and its precarious quiver. There is a poetic beauty in its motion, in the snap that shakes it top to bottom, but I don't like the way it trembles, threatening to quit at any moment.

So this is the seat of passion. The alleged well of all emotion. An organ arrested to every pale poet's cheapest conceit. But to stand beside the heart is to feel its force, its power. To taste its darkest, richest, blackest blood.

I reach out and touch the heart, which has been beating since before I was born; a certainty behind my breast which has always quickened to see you coming. Something inside which I have sensed and felt, but never seen. Like a mysterious instrument, it calls me closer, it entices me to pluck its strings, to sound out its hollow parts. It dares me to turn it on its side and tap it, drawing out the low tones of its familiar echo.

'Lysette, Lysette, Lysette, I can feel that there is love in here—'

No. Stop it. I must maintain my composure.

—But how can I ignore how cleanly and completely it empties and refills itself, demonstrating the true simplicity of love – an inward, outward, inward flow. I kiss the blunted tip which quivers near a rib, and am convinced that here I witness something perfect, a thing designed for love.

I pull myself away from gazing on the heart, as I now intend to move inside of it, careful of any damage I may unwittingly inflict. Under the first fold of heart skin I find evidence of early sorrows, and beneath the deeper folds lie the reminders of more serious pains. My fingers brush the rough edges of an old scar, small in size, but sharp and deep. This is Jonnie's death, and the damage is not so bad as I imagined it – a serious wound, true; but it seems well healed. Although encrusted with tissue, the section remains beautifully functional.

Using the penknife I carry in my pocket, I cut away the edges of the scar and let the pink tissue beneath it breathe. Suddenly I cut too close and a little blood leaks out. I staunch the flow by poking my finger into the hole, and the heart swells up around it, beating fast to hold it closed. With a silver needle and a golden thread, I close the new incision with smooth and careful stitches, and even Miss Fickle would have to admire my handiwork.

With this damage fixed, I am able to move deeper into the heart's dark interior. I step into the stream of blood which carries me to an inner chamber; an unchartered region, unmarked on any map or diagram. Once inside, something rattles above me with an almost wooden sound. Trembling, I look up to the dome of the highest heart wall, which vaults above me like the spire of a cathedral. Squinting in the darkness, I can see that the walls are lined with shadowy images.

I step a little closer and squint my eyes, realising that the largest image is a picture of you, Lysette. It is your portrait I see, hanging inside the heart within my heart. Yours is the image I hang highest; yours is the one I take down and dust most often, the one most waxed and shined by my sleeve, the one most buffeted by my breath. You are the one I take out every day to gaze upon. The one I hold in my hand and clutch close to my soul, the one I smile over, the one most stained by my tears, the one I handle and put back as carefully as if I handled sacred glass.

I realise suddenly that I must be capable of love. No. Much more than that. I have loved with such depth that the results of that love have been stitched into the fabric of my heart. Every face has been sewn into the skin, and every name must be whispered on each drop of blood which passes through my body.

I admire the gallery of bright and smiling faces hanging on the walls. Your face is the brightest, but there are others too who are enshrined alongside you: Jonnie, with her sun-dappled freckles and lop-sided grin, for here she still lives; here she can never get older and will never die. Agnes, stern and commanding, but with a knowing fire behind her eyes. Father, gruff and pipe-smoking, but patient with his books and maps, teaching me mathematics as I sit upon his lap. My mother too, for I can remember her here. She is a tall, fair, slim young woman, cradling me as a baby in her arms, cooing and clucking and delighting in my tooth-less smile, and kissing my soft brown baby curls, which remind her of my father. Here also is a student from years ago who brought me flowers and oranges and gave me a pair of fine gloves one Christmas. Even the Hambleton chil-dren have a place inside my heart; they who squeal and play beneath my window, and I look down and wish them well. But most of all you, Lysette, you are the centre of my heart, the image around which all the other images turn.

I kneel down carefully in the soft, fig-shaped pit of my heart and pray for a second chance. 'Please, let me return. Let me rouse myself from this strange dream, let me return to my life, and I promise, this time I will do it properly. Not only will I love Lysette, I will love her more than reason, more than what is prudent, much more than what would be proper between a friend and her friend. And this time, I will be wiser. I will value this resilient piece of muscle, I will never doubt its power, and I will hold it safe inside my chest.'

I can feel the slowing and softening of the walls around me and above my head, and I know my time inside is com-ing to an end. I feel the need to savour each remaining moment as the force of the blood flow diminishes and trickles away. I discover a nice warm spot within the boundaries of the heart's blunt shadow, and there I sit quietly, admiring the small blue flowers that sprout around the shadow's edge. *'Oh please, oh please, give me the strength to endure whatever must come next. Please, if nothing else, simply let me see Lysette.'*

PART FIVE

'. . . nor are those empty-hearted whose low sounds
reverb no hollowness . . .'

King Lear

CHAPTER TEN

It doesn't take me long to realise that something remarkable has happened; that in fact, I haven't died. It is early morning and the day dawns all around me, seeping into my brain along with the light that floods my eyelids, and the bitter liquid which fills my mouth. A misty grey-green light inches through the window, finding the furniture, colouring the carpets, waking the plants and extinguishing the last of the evening's ghosts and lurking terrors. How strange and distant all my griefs seem now. I feel the warmth rising through the floorboards as the bakery ovens heat up beneath me, and the Hambleton children stir and cry as they rise, bleary-eyed, from bed.

'Lysette. Lysette.' Her name is the first word to rise from my lips. 'Lysette, I must tell you something wonderful. But first I must find you and bring you back home.' *Oh please, oh please, let this not be a dream. Let this be real. If it be so, it is a chance which does redeem all sorrow that ever I have felt.* I rise from bed amazed at my lightness; amazed at the silvery quickness of my skin. I slip into some clothes, which glide easily over my body, a body which can no longer be confined by ties or hems or buttons. I feel a thrilling tapping in my limbs, and an excited quiver that echoes through my neck and chest. A new refrain settles into my mind as I throw open my window and look down dizzily into the busy street beneath me. *The day, my friends, and all things stay, for me.* There can be no excuse for wasting time now, not while I live, and Lysette waits for me, somewhere on the other side of London; she waits, and has not been told yet today of the depths of my love for her.

I slip down the narrow steel staircase and into the dusty, lovely, yeast-scented streets, where boys play with balls and sticks and little girls in pinafores skip and squeal with delight. Sleek black motorcars whiz past me at fourteen miles per hour, nearly tipping me with their errant breezes. I am so free, so unencumbered; so dazzling with joy that I skip on tiptoe and wave my cap at the peddlers and the magazine vendors, who shake their tins of coins and smile at me and at each other, scratching their heads as if there is something unusual in seeing a grown woman dancing down the street.

I quickly reach Kestrel Close, and am surprised at how ordinary Lysette's house appears. It seems that so much more time has to have passed by now, and surely the world must have changed as much as I have. Lysette's roof should be barren of bricks, the walls should have fallen, and the garden path should be treacherous, overgrown with decay. I expect, at the very least, a sign to be posted on the door saying 'This is a house full of unhappiness, and I have packed up and moved somewhere else.' But the windowsill has been recently dusted, and the brass door knocker shines in the light.

I open the garden gate and the lock tumbles with the good solid sound of certainty, and droplets of hope and desire fall through my body. I notice that the vines around the window are higher than the last time I was here. My mouth runs hot with wanting. *Oh, Lysette, let us leave this place, let us not tarry one minute more, for we have wasted far too much time already*. I stand beneath Lysette's window, reed-voiced and wooing with more hope than bravado. I hold my cap in my hand as my fingers quiver.

'*Lysette*,' I call out. '*Lysette, please come to the door. It's Tranby, dear, I'm here*.' Hearing no reply, I enter the house through the unlocked door, my senses drinking in everything I see: Lysette's silver hairbrush, spidered with swirls of her hair; her high-buttoned boots, bent at an anxious angle under the table; a dish of dry cake with raspberry jam, crowned with crumbs in the shape of her lips. A chipped teacup on a saucer, inked with a stain of dried tea. A flutter of stamps, a trail of penny blacks leading from the desk to the floor. A fountain pen, pregnant with colour, resting heavily on its side, threatening the pure white doily beneath.

I move quickly, slipping from room to room. Lysette is in the bedroom, curled up on her side. She is completely quiet. I see a large bump poking up on her shoulder, and a dried flower of brown blood blooms on the pillowcase beneath her pale, parted lips. *No, Lysette, no, we are about to go away. This is no time for you to die*. As I step closer, I can feel that she is still breathing, but only barely. Her gentle breaths make me feel faint. I touch her forehead and she blinks as I wipe out the corners of her swollen eyes. She lies back and lets me be her ministering angel as her shoulders slip deep into the sheets.

'Tranby, come back Tranby,' she whispers, having no idea how close her wish is to reality. *Yes, dear, yes. Relax, Love. I'm here.*

Lysette is injured, but she will survive. She will live and heal enough to be beaten by her husband again. I wish more than anything that I had the courage to kill him. I am tempted to step out into the street to look for him, to find him in his drunken stupor with his scalp sweating and his tight necktie burning his skin, as he laughs and sings and slaps other men across the back. I wish I could cut his throat, or toss him in the filthy river, leaving him to be fished out by beggars or mudlarks, with his body so decayed that even the resurrection men would refuse his foul-smelling corpse, and allow him to wash up further downstream on the cold and feeble beaches of the Thames.

'Tranby, Tranby, please come back to me,' Lysette says, summoning me up from behind her eyelids, and I vow to stay at her side. I'll abide with her this evening, wrap my arms around her and protect her through the night.

Malcolm returns after midnight. He has been drinking, and his heavy steps echo through the house like a fearful, trembling pulse that shakes in my ears and makes me want to hide my head in the pillow. He sings rough Scots songs in a fractured tempo, sour music that stiffens the walls of this room. I hear him ascend the staircase and I duck beneath the bed. He opens the door and faint light falls across the floor. He takes a few steps towards the bed, then stops. He carries a kerosene lamp and I can smell fruited pomade in his sweat-dampened hair. He stands only long enough to settle his dizziness and convince himself that Lysette is still alive, still breathing beneath the bloody sheets. I hear him move to the study and groan. He throws the full weight of his body on the long sofa which buckles, swaying beneath him. In a matter of seconds he is asleep and snoring like a winded pig. Dear God, I want to kill him. I could go into that room and do it now, I could hold a pillow over his bloated red face until the struggle stops. I consider it, but then I remember Lysette, her shrouded eyes and the pain carved around her mouth, and I know how much I need to stay beside her, I know how fully she alone is the only thing for which I returned to life.

The next morning Malcolm wakes early and I hear him produce copious amounts of sour green urine. He rubs his face until his beard is raw, then he cooks some eggs and sits down to some bookkeeping in his study.

Lysette still sleeps, but her breathing is easier and her skin is warm. *Soon, Lysette, soon. When you awake, we will flee. Arise, and quit this place of sadness.* I prepare to tell her adventure stories, whispered fantasies that should arouse her ear, break into her brain and prevent it from sleeping. She has always loved adventure stories, but now, as I set to spin some, as I trace the rim of her ear with my finger, I rake my imagination and find it empty. Months ago I might have begun by saying, 'When de Bougainville first saw Tahiti,' or 'There is a golden canopy in India, a massive tent astride the river Ganges, beneath which only women live, and freedom flows like honey . . .' but now I have seen both this world and the next, and my stories are bankrupt, have lost the power to delight. 'What sad little lives we had led,' I tell her. 'Reality was in Camberwell all along.'

By three o'clock Lysette is shaking and feverish. I am careful to air out the sheets at hourly intervals, to make sure the scent of death does not settle itself too near her nose. Her eyelids quiver occasionally, and she tries to speak. I am as anxious as a moth fluttering above her lips. I live to hear her gentle sigh, to see her chest move up and down. I wish now that I had lived my whole life only as this being. A thing radiant but feathered with hope.

Suddenly I hear Malcolm moving down the corridor. I slide behind the curtain as he enters the room. He is still drunk, but less afraid than before. His stiff white collar is open and his shirtsleeves are rolled up to his meaty red elbows. He moves to the bed and lifts Lysette in his arms. He hurts her now without meaning to – his hands are hard; rough and heavy, and his heart is brutal too. I can feel the brute force of it, rattling like a madman in his chest, pounding to get out. He lets Lysette fall back to the bed. He hates what he has done to her and knows he is likely to do it again. I pity him too much to hate him any more. He leaves the room and goes downstairs. In a few minutes I hear the door slam, and I slip to the window and see him in his dark coat as he hunkers down the street. I hope he'll be gone for ever. I indulge in the thought that he might never return. He drank all the claret from the study, and then finished off the whisky, and I imagine he'll drink gin in the pot-house down the road, then continue on to The Falcon Arms, where he can enjoy himself shooting pigeons, watching cock-fights, and cheering for wiry little dogs that capture thin rats in their bloody jaws.

Lysette whimpers, and nearly wakes up before slipping back into sleep. Her eyes are hurt by the pale, dusty light seeping through the crack in the heavy velvet curtains. She catches her breath in surprise at the pain in her chest, which her fingers search for but can't quite pin down. I stroke her forehead, soothing her with my touch. *'Shhh, my darling. Rest, I am here with you. I will never again let you go.'*

Evening encroaches, swallowing the room's final flitting light. *'Lysette. Please. Wake up. Arise, and we will leave this place.'* I light the candles made of pure yellow beeswax and then I light a small rolled pastille to disinfect the room. I fold my hands in prayer as I kneel at the side of the bed, clasping the white sheets to steady myself. Lysette is better, and Malcolm has not returned. These are gifts to be grateful for. I have dressed Lysette in a clean chemise, fresh drawers and a soft bonnet, and tucked her under fresh-pressed bed linen. I have put double stockings on her feet to warm her toes, and a pillow underneath her legs to ease the blood flow back to her heart. Her face is relaxed, her lips no longer swollen. I have doused the room with perfume and arranged flowers so she can not avoid them, the minute that her eyes first open. I have hung marigolds and daisies and unripened violets, which might stimulate her with their scent. *'Lord, look after my lovely Lysette. Never let her doubt how much I love her. Let me have the chance to love her, better, one more time. Let the world be kind to her, for she will repay that kindness a thousand fold. Spare her from iniquity, she's had too much of that already. My dearest wish is that you protect her gentle heart from sorrow.'*

'Oh, Tranby. Don't be sad for me. I'm beginning to feel so much better,' she says.

My eyes fly open. The room is altered, one shade darker now, one degree nearer to nighttime. Lysette is motionless. 'See how she dreams about me,' I whisper to myself.

'Tranby, please. I'm not dreaming. I've heard every word you've said.'

Hair rises on the back of my neck. Liquid slips through my body. I reach out to touch her. Her eyes are closed, but her lips are moving. Satisfaction plays at the muscles in her face.

'Lysette – can you hear me? Do you know that I am here?' I ask.

She opens her eyes. At first she looks past me, but then her gaze hardens and she stares into my face, and I can see my own face reflected in her eyes. 'Of course,' she says wearily, pulling loose the strings of the bonnet. 'I've known you were here since yesterday. When you came into the room, it was as if I could feel you creeping into my heart.'

I sit down beside her on the bed. 'Come closer, dear, and let me love you,' she commands, wrapping her arms around me and pressing her fists into my back. I put my arms around her, and I am surprised at how precisely she fits me, how exactly my bones recall all our previous embraces. My fingers brush the lump which rises up near her spine. She winces, drawing in a deep draught of pain.

'I am sorry,' I murmur and my voice resonates in my throat before catching damply in the strands of her hair, where I can feel and taste it, right before my eyes.

'You've been on an amazing journey, Tranby Quirke,' she tells me, and her voice vibrates against my neck.

'Yes,' I say, pulling back in surprise. 'I have. But how did you know that?'

'I can see it in your eyes. In your face, in your features,' she says.

'What do you see?' I ask with excitement that the change in me is so profound as to be written on my skin.

'You look older. But I mean that as a good thing. Wiser. Radiant. Settled, in some way. As if you've been blessed with a special knowledge. You've been some place very far away.'

I am amazed at her perception. 'Yes,' I answer. 'Lysette, I want to tell you all about it, but I'm not certain if I can find the proper words.'

'Don't worry. I'm far too tired to listen now. Tell me tomorrow. When we leave London,' she whispers, as her eyelids slide closed. 'There will be time to tell me everything.'

'That I do promise you,' I answer, kissing her cheek with all the purposed honesty I can muster. Lysette sinks under the blankets, struggling to get comfortable. She pulls down the rising edge of her chemise and smoothes away a wrinkle. She slips off the bonnet and runs her fingers through her hair, separating a few small knots. Her fingers catch, and her eyes narrow as if she's upset by her messiness. I long to grab a brush from her bedside console and brush her hair until it shines in the candlelight, until it glows like spun fire, throwing bright sparks from the crisp centre part, but instead I clasp Lysette's body deep in the middle of the bed. I am afraid of letting her go, afraid she might disappear even in the narrow reaches of the sheets. I turn down the top blanket so she can breathe more easily. She is already dreaming. I close my eyes to keep the tears locked inside me. I am not yet ready to let them fall from my face and splash against her body, not while the renewed softness of my heart assaults me, beating quick beneath my skin.

My darling Lysette – Let this be my last midnight writing. From now on, all our journeys will be blessed by truth and daylight. Today we shall be married, in your sitting room at two o'clock this very afternoon. Before that time we will bathe in milk, and then in perfume. You'll prepare your most expensive fragrances from France, pouring them out like bath water, until our eyes and our pores and our secret places burn from the richness of the priceless fluids, and with little china teacups we will anoint one another in the bathtub, trickling the liquid over our damp and fragrant heads.

Then you'll choose our bridal clothing. For me, you pick a long white nightdress, insisting that I wear white because I am more the maiden than yourself. You dress me carefully, and I have a vision of the joys I missed in womanhood, in being dressed and combed, paper-curled and sweetly scented. You fix a petticoat under my gown, padding it out with a horsehair and linen crinoline, and cinch it tight at my waist. You weave me a ribbon and flower headpiece, and for yourself you alter a high society, cream-coloured tea gown with a long fluted bustle that trails evenly along the floor.

Next you sit me at the vanity table with your cosmetic colours and Viennese powders; the eyebrow pencil, the lip-salve, the powder puff and rouge pot, and you use them to dress my face. How easily my sallowness disappears, skirted under streaks of pinks and reds. 'Kiss me, you fool,' you plead, grabbing my face in your hands. I begin to kiss you, planting a million kisses up and down your arms, covering your shoulders and plastering your chin. I bestow so many kisses that your body becomes a map, and the kisses are the signposts by which I plot the path of love.

We drape flowers and small garlands everywhere, and devise a little trellis under which we walk arm in arm. The details make it real, for this is no girlish play-time fantasy. We fill the house with rice, and paper birds; wax candles in each corner, and music from the phonograph; rich, sweet sounds that pour out of the fluted golden horn. You bring out the silver dishes kept hot by spirit lamps; the devilled kidneys, the baked ham, the ptarmigan, and the cold roast pheasant, meats so heavy they threaten to overturn the hardwood table. The kitchen smells of game hens boiling in heavy brown gravy, and a Christmas plum pudding sitting boldly on the silver serving tray has been released early from its dish of dark red rum. Bright quivering jellies and stalks of preserved fruit float in jars of coloured glass beside the boxes of round cream biscuits, stacked evenly on commemorative coronation dishes.

You open the windows and let the birds fly in to be our witnesses, along with a few blond baby dolls dug up from your hope chest, and last of all, straining with both arms, you haul in a granite idol from the garden, a smiling pug-nosed elf, to oversee our wedding, to serve us both as priest and witness.

You walk me down our makeshift aisle – a long damask silk tablecloth lining the hardwood floor. As you pace out the steps beneath your breath, I try to apologise.

'Lysette, I'm sorry I betrayed you at the station,' I say, but we are at the altar now, and you bow your head and clasp my hand, and I am silent as your tongue proclaims the inner promise of our love. 'Tranby, Lysette; Tranby, Lysette; Tranby, Lysette,' you recite, and our vows require no more words than these.

When the ceremony ends, you let the music play again as you take me in your arms, waltzing across the festively decorated room. I attempt to assault you with my apologies, feeling I must make sense of my regrets, but you prevent it. 'I've forgiven you,' you say simply, dancing faster, holding my cheek against your chest. You press my face into your body so I may not speak, and my penitence remains unheard, absolved and soon forgotten, lost in the softness of your breast. 'I've forgiven you for everything. You came back to me from the ends of the earth. What more could I ask of you than that?'

Night falls and we move towards making love. 'Let this be our first time as married lovers,' you pledge, leading me to the bed which has been especially prepared for this evening, stuffed with pillows and tied all around with satin ribbons. 'You and I are married now, we are sworn guardians to each other's souls,' you say solemnly. We make love following your instructions. The pleasure is intense and somewhat melancholy, and we cling tightly to each other as if fearing we may disappear the moment the sun muscles in, parting the curtains and splitting the window, dancing eerily across the hardwood floor. I am praying for a cloudy day, hoping we may disappear simply, enveloped in a looming balloon of dull yellow fog. If it is cloudy, I can say I am leaving London on a day most sympathetic to the way I lived, allowing me the chance to bid good-bye to the chilly, damp, and soulless elements which were my siblings, surrounded by the lifeless things I wrongly loved so much.

A rough rattle shakes the room, pulling me away from my dream. Lysette turns over, thinking I'm getting up. She holds to my thigh, but I reassure her, 'I'm still here, Lysette.' Then we hear the door slam closed and know that Malcolm has come home.

'Hide,' Lysette says. 'It's Malcolm. Hide before he sees you,' she insists.

'No,' I tell her. 'I will not hide. I don't want to be invisible any longer. Lysette, I lived my whole life hiding from someone or something. Now I want to shout aloud how much I love you.'

The door flies open. Malcolm considers the two of us lying in the bed, holding hands and trying to steady each other's tremors.

His face turns pale with shock and indignation. Then suddenly he begins to laugh. 'Well, this isn't the man I expected to find in my bed,' he says. 'I knew you were unfaithful, but with a woman? A little woman who thinks she can be a man. Have you figured out how to keep my wife happy? Bless you if you manage it, satisfying this trussed-up little tart with the poison patch between her legs.'

Malcolm comes nearer to the bed and flutters some papers in our faces. 'Do you know what these are? Tickets. For the train to Edinburgh, and on to Inverness. Train tickets, and three hundred pounds. We're leaving tomorrow to spend three months in the Highlands,' he says gleefully.

'I'll not go with you,' Lysette says, rising from the sheets like a white-armed apparition. 'I'd rather die than go anywhere with you.'

'We shall see about that,' he says, pushing her to the bed. Straddling her with his knees, he fumbles with his trousers. I grab his shoulder, desperately trying to fight him off.

'You're going to stop me? You?' he asks with a snicker. 'Not bloody likely.' He pushes me away and leans back to throw a punch, but I twirl out of his reach. 'Why, you little . . .' he says, lunging towards me. The fire in his eyes frightens me, and I believe he means to kill us both. Suddenly I notice the huge brass candlestick near the window, and I feel the power surging inside me, knowing that at last I have the courage to kill him.

Malcolm is behind Lysette, twisting her arm behind her back, as her spine curls and her face squeezes scarlet. He pushes her against the wall and punches her hard in the chest. I hear the snap of her ribs breaking, and as she falls, she hits her head against the bedside table, catching the corner of it near her ear.

I grab the candlestick and lunge at Malcolm. As he turns towards me, I close my eyes and direct all my strength to my arm, thinking that in a moment we will be free.

The candlestick comes crashing down, landing only a glancing blow to the side of Malcolm's head, but it is enough to stun him and bring him to his knees.

'Lysette, I've done it!' I shout, but Lysette says nothing. She lies quiet on the floor. I kneel, supporting her head while her eyes glaze over. I pull her carefully into my lap, cradling her close to my chest. 'No, Lysette. Please be all right. This wasn't supposed to happen,' I say, holding her tightly.

'Tranby, don't be frightened. Just say again that you love me,' she asks as her fingers dance across my arm.

'I do love you. More than anything in the world,' I tell her as I stroke her cheek which is dampened by a few pink tears.

'Good. Then all shall be well,' she says and sighs.

Suddenly the morning sun rides through the window, and the bright hot rays settle on Lysette, motionless in a ring of quiet blood. I sit and still myself, ready to grab the hem of impending doom, wishing it would come now, right now, wishing it would gallop in on a roaring white horse. I don't hear any approaching hoofbeats. The only sound is Malcolm weeping softly in the corner, and I look over my shoulder and see his heavy hands balancing the weight of his face. I cannot bear this an instant longer. Please, come and get me; please take me, please swallow me whole, and do it now, right now. Lysette is fading, she is fading, but I refuse to let her go; not until I feel her soul rising and floating away from me, lifting from her lips like the flutter of a dozen birds.

PART SIX

'. . . Death, once dead, there's no more dying then.'

Sonnet CXLVI

CHAPTER ELEVEN

My darling, darling, darling Lysette – You are sleeping beside me and I write my words following the rhythm of your breathing, mimicking that steady ebb and flow. My free hand stays watchman to your pulse. I feel the beat of blood but barely dare believe it, that you are real and alive and right here by my side. I watch the world fly by outside my window; at fifty-five miles per hour we are on the Flying Scotsman, hurtling headlong towards Edinburgh on the fastest train in the world.

The jarring motion tosses and turns your wounded insides, so I wrap around you, holding you still. 'All will be well,' I tell you as I tip back the wide brim of your hat and a long shadow crosses your face, keeping the bright sun out of your eyes.

Let me quickly explain the situation. I feared you were dead, Lysette. An awful silence had filled the room, and your cheeks were pale as marble. I cried in a way I never had before, but then a strange thing happened – something told me not to fear; you were not dead, you simply slept, and I could kiss you back to consciousness. 'But she is so still,' I insisted, holding up your thin pale arm, which was limp from the lack of blood running through it. Your face was silent, and no beauty bloomed beneath your eyes. But then, in an act of reckless abandon, I had the courage to believe this little voice inside me, so I threw all convention to hell and lifted you in my arms and kissed you, letting my blood rush into your body. For a moment we were as one creature. I felt the earth buckle beneath me; and realised this is an earth capable of, but not often asked to perform, such wondrous things. Your chest heaved painfully. Your face was broken, shattered like fine china teacups, and the tiny veins revealed the fissures spreading through your skull. Your eyes opened on lightness and white-hot pain, and your pupils narrowed, attempting to take it all in. I felt you struggle as awareness rose through your body.

'Tranby, Tranby, I thought I was dead,' you said, lifting your hand to your chest, but I told you to be still and quiet, because I would care for you, and you mustn't worry, because you were only dreaming anyway.

And this is what happened next. I held you in my arms, and my heart and brain were racing. I saw the door of chance slide open, and a new world beckoned us in. I made a deal with Malcolm, who was sitting in the corner. These events had changed him into a small, lopsided man whose rough red eyes, fresh from weeping, had seen more than his body could believe. He looked incapable of hurting anyone.

'You will do as I say,' I told him firmly. 'Tomorrow morning you will go to Scotland Yard and tell the police that a small dark man broke into your house, stole three hundred pounds and kidnapped your wife. You will say you tried to fight him off, but he hit you with a candlestick and knocked you unconscious.' I looked at the bright purple bruise astride Malcolm's broad head, which he balanced on his fingertips as if holding a delicate flower. 'You will tell them that as the man left, you heard him threatening to kill Lysette, strip her naked and throw her dead body into the Thames if she did not do as he told her. When the police find Lysette's clothing by the river they will believe this story, and the bruise on your head will serve as evidence. The story of a businessman will always be believed. They will never find her body, but in this weather, they will not expect to; in fact they will not search unduly long. You will be left a widower with wealth and prospects, and you will have the sympathy of respectable people. You will be able to marry again, marry a woman who will give you many healthy sons.' I related the tale as quickly as it unfolded in my imagination.

'And you?' he asked wearily, looking up at me with an expression of bewilderment that bordered on respect.

'You will never think about either of us again,' I answered confidently. 'Consider us invisible. Consider us dead. Consider us as dust on the wind, but whatever you do, do not dwell on us until your dying day, when, on your deathbed, you will bless Lysette and Tranby for giving you a chance for another life.'

'Two hundred pounds,' he said softly, shaking his head.

'What?' I asked, not understanding what he meant.

'I'll give you two hundred pounds. Not three. She isn't worth three. Take your two hundred and we've a deal.'

'Give me two hundred and fifty, and the tickets,' I demanded.

'Fair enough,' he said, and I accepted, and as we shook hands, I realised I was touching the hand of the man who had first purchased you, Lysette, and who had somehow made our escape both possible and, perhaps, inevitable.

Then we left that horrible, wretched, miserable little life. I threw some things into a suitcase, grabbed some of Malcolm's clothes; his tights, his linen shirts, his thin muslin handkerchiefs, and we stole away from your husband's house as swift as two thieves in the night, but I knew I had captured a rich and valuable jewel, something as precious as life itself. You, still woozy, balanced against my arm, and our hearts were beating hard as we trudged through the early morning mist, and as we neared the bridge I could not resist running the last few yards. Imagine my delight in realising that, yes, it can be done. A grown woman can run, you were right about that fact. Ladies are able to propel their bodies forward, but only if we throw all caution to the wind and allow ourselves the freedom to fly.

And so we came upon the River Thames in chilly early morning light and found it shining with unearthly brightness. The air was sharp and frigid, pummelling our lungs, but the water was warm and surprisingly buoyant, as I dipped my elbow in to check the temperature.

'It's fine, Lysette,' I reassured you. We watched the water bubble up around the banks. This was a tide without force or fury, a tide content to stay near the shore and keep us company. The foam that tickled our fingers was frothy and as soft as lace. I carefully undressed you, mentally preparing diagrams of your bruises, while I calculated how much love you would need in order to be completely healed.

We crouched under the shadow of the wooden bridge and I held you in the surf, and you were as pale as a newborn infant. I washed away the blood and dirt, and found the fresh bruises beneath the skin, but you did not cry, you did not complain, and I could not resist kissing your hands and neck and wrists. We heard the rattle of wooden carts and men on horseback overhead and that sound echoed deep inside our chests, where we suppressed our laughter until long after we were sure we were alone again.

The water had some healing properties, warmed as it was by both the pull of the moon and the pulse of our bodies, and as I swept my lips across the surface I found it tasted both sweet and salty, clear and fishless, as if it were composed only of the joyful tears of spirits, drifting through the clouds and weeping overhead.

I removed my clothes and laid them out carefully along the shoreline. Then before I stepped into the water I considered my body, the one I'd hated all these thirty-four years, and never had it looked so fine and beautiful. I noticed how my ribs were curved and even, visible beneath the skin, my narrow thighs were hinged with perfect kneecaps, and I could feel a ring of strong muscles tightening in my upper arm. As I slipped into the river, my small breasts blossomed, rounded and buoyed by the water.

I took you in with me to the deeper part of the river, near the centre, and I balanced your body on top of mine. I wore you like a shield, like a proud and naked thing to flaunt the sky.

'You look silver, Tranby,' you said. 'It must be the sunlight. Look how sleek and sharp you appear, my sweet beautiful saviour.' I considered my hands and wrists and feet, glinting brightly beneath the water, and I was thinking the very same thing.

'Let's love one another,' you suggested, pushing away, then paddling back towards me as your hair swelled and darkened on the surface of the river.

'Why not?' I asked. 'Let's start right away. Let's not waste an instant.' So we climbed out on the cold riverbank and had a quick tryst on our knees in the damp sand; a love full of soft hands and blunted tongues, with much kneeling and touching, and feather caresses; and we stayed mindful of bruises as we probed each other with thumbs, the way we might consider the skin of a palpable apple. Everything ached a little, but with our bodies solid again the pain was as intense and as lasting as the beauty, and when our breath came together and lengthened in one long flow, it was easy to look out on the river, and feel another river flowing soft and dark inside us, and to know this was the beginning and the end of many things. Even if we lived a thousand years, some part of us would always remain here, on the edges of the River Thames.

We dressed quickly, hiding behind our clothes like first-time lovers suddenly struck shy. We slipped into our new identities, and rolled our old clothes into a ball and set them free upon the water. We waved good-bye to those lives as our damp stringy things floated like dark thoughts downstream, and for dramatic effect I hung your corset, your garter, and your gloves over the bridge rail as a marker, as a guide to lead the police to the lie that would set us free.

Then we hired a taxi motorcar to hurry us to the station, and after I gave our driver a ten-shilling tip, we boarded this train to Edinburgh, and there has been no sign of Malcolm, or the police; no, not even so much as a glimmer of Miss Wilhelmina Fickle. I look around the carriage at the many people drinking tea and talking and playing cards, and I realise that no one here could possibly care who we are, where we go, or what we do. Smiling people surround us on every side, as bright and lively as birds, and I can feel the quickening of their hearts from across the aisle seats.

Looking out of the window, I notice that we have just passed Sheffield. I tick off the names of the passing towns like a list of fond and well-considered friends; Doncaster, Leeds, Darlington, and Durham. We are more than half-way to Edinburgh, where our new lives will begin; where I will love you come what may, where I will love you more than reason, more than what is prudent, much more than what is proper between a friend and her friend. The ticket master barrels through our carriage. I hand him our tickets and he never sees our faces as he punches the paper and smiles to the leather emptiness above our heads.

You sigh as I write this – I suspect several of your ribs are broken. I have secured you in a corset, but I've left the whalebone frame unhooked in the front and instead I've wrapped the laces loosely all around, to hold your torso still. I think this image is appropriate, for if we women have risen from the broken rib of Adam, that break is mended now in our own lives. At the place where we heal into each other, there will be no mark, no scar, and no proof that we were ever more or less than one body, one form.

I have stolen an apple from the costermonger at the market stall and I will work it into a paste to ease over your torn lip and broken teeth. It will take time to heal you, but time is the one luxury left to us now. Our new lives will be hard at first, and we must be honest about that. We will dress in bonnets and shawls. We will never look up, and never speak unless spoken to. But no one will notice us, and invisibility is suddenly a wonderful gift. Consider this: I am old and homely. You are young, but burdened with a barren body and a broken face. No one would want us now, and our lips are sealed with our secret. And when the world least expects it of us, we will board that ferry to France, and once across the Channel, we will purchase our own motorcar, light fistfuls of long, elegant cigarettes, and go roaring wildly through Parisian streets. The broad-minded

French will allow us a lifetime of love, and when we reach eighty or ninety or one hundred years old, young people will laugh at us, considering us doddery, or odd. A few people will look at us and think, 'Something not quite natural there, something about them is not quite right.' But then they will pass by, and not notice how we smile to ourselves, content in the memory of our sixty-year love.

But that will all come much, much later. For many years, beginning this very afternoon, we will lead a secret life. Did we have to spurn the world to make it possible? Yes, perhaps, but that is a sacrifice I will embrace. To love you, ultimately, is enough.

You draw a sharp breath as you turn in your seat. I must stop writing, stop for ever, and devote the next few months to making you well. The pain still hovers above your face. Glancing at you now, I can trace the progress as the shadow passes over you, tightening your cheek, lining your forehead, rubbing black ash deep into the corner of your eye. I loosen the corset lace around your chest and you breathe more easily. This is the work of my womanhood, discovered at an advanced, but not too late, age: to love, protect, and heal. Your breathing quickens and I pause my pen—

—I imagine our lives will be so precious and precarious from this day forward. We will always be looking over our shoulders, into the past, true; but also into the future. We shall not fear death, having seen what we have seen. We shall live simply, and simply live. Here let me offer up my new vows, my devotions for an honest life. I will not read novels. I will not daydream of adventuresome travels. I will not teach young women to lead their lives by lies. I will do no more, no less, than this: I will love you for ever, Lysette. And this time, I will love you better.

Your eyes open. You whisper my name. 'Tranby? Tranby? Where . . .?'

'Shh,' I tell you. 'Shhhhhhhh. Stay quiet, darling. All is well. I've nearly finished writing now. Take only shallow breaths, Lysette. Take only shallow breaths. Yes, Lysette, yes. We are born again, 'tis true. And I shall only love.'